PILGRIMS AND PIONEERS: NEW ENGLAND WOMEN IN THE ARTS

PILGRIMS AND PIONEERS: NEW ENGLAND WOMEN IN THE ARTS

Edited by
Alicia Faxon
and
Sylvia Moore

Midmarch Arts Press
New York, 1987

MIDMARCH ARTS BOOKS

Guide to Women's Art Organizations and Directory for the Arts

Voices of Women: 3 Critics on 3 Poets on 3 Heroines

Women Artists of the World

American Women Artists: Works on Paper

Library of Congress Catalog Card Number: 87-060021
ISBN 0-9602476-6-1

To place an order, write:
Midmarch Arts
Box 3304
Grand Central Station
New York, NY 10163

DEDICATION

According to a National Endowment for the Arts study, between 1970 and 1980 the number of women artists increased by 162 percent. While women artists represent 38 percent of all artists, their work is shown only 10 percent of the time in mainstream institutions.[1] Meanwhile, women artists have been actively putting themselves on the record, making themselves visible, uncovering their history. To be in history is to have a name, to be recognized, to be in a context, for without context women artists are anomalies. As noted, feminist work has often been received as if it emerged from nowhere; as if each of us had lived, thought, and worked without any historical past or contextual present.[2]

Looking into the mirror of society, and finding it empty, women artists have experienced a sense of dislocation. Now, as women's art networks grow, we are creating a society where women are acknowledged as creators. This book is a testament to our effort.

— **Sarah Sutro**, Boston

Notes:
1. *Women and Minorities in Artist Occupations*, National Endowment for the arts, Research Division, Note 4 (July 4, 1983).
2. Adrienne Rich, *On Lies, Secrets, and Silence*. (New York: W.W. Norton & Co., 1979) p.11.

CONTENTS

PREFACE

The idea for this book was suggested by Cynthia Navaretta, publisher/editor of *Women Artists News*, to honor New England women artists on the occasion of the Women's Caucus for Art and College Art Association meeting in Boston, February, 1987. Contributors are all from the New England area and familiar with the terrain, its joys and sorrows. The book became a collaboration of New England artists, historians, and museum and gallery people, and represents, in fact, the overall women's art community in the region. As all do not all come from the same background, several points of view are given, a variety that expresses the ongoing vitality and diversity of the Boston group in particular. One thing, however, unites all contributors— a deep conviction about the importance of women's art and a strong desire to make it known.

Most of the material is completely original and never before published. It is the result of patient research, many interviews and many visits to museums, historical societies and studios. The papers and diaries of women artists of the past have been studied, as well as their art.

What do we find when we look at the work of New England women? First, a fiercely independent group of individuals searching for new and pertinent ways to express their vision. This is as true for the women sculptors who went to Rome in the nineteenth century as for contemporary New England women artists. Related to the art of their own time stylistically and conceptually, and working with sophisticated techniques, today's women make equally strong personal statements.

Another characteristic is a feminist perception and conceptual system. Although it would usually be impossible to specify the gender of the creator, there is often a strand of awareness of women's orientation in both nineteenth and twentieth century work that expresses, as Edmonia Lewis put it, the point of view of "all women who have struggled and suffered."

One of the interesting themes, particularly in twentieth century work, is an awareness of space. The tensions between explorations of inner and outer space and between inward and outward vision are explored in several essays.

Both in the nineteenth and twentieth century New England women have made political statements in their art— Hosmer, Lewis, and Whitney in the nineteenth century, and many twentieth century women. In this they are similar to sister artists throughout the world. Besides political statements in their art that may or may not be feminist in orientation, women artists, often treated as a minority or powerless group, have been acutely aware of the politics of the art world. They have been rejected by juries, galleries, museums, and potential patrons on the basis of gender rather than quality. An awareness of this bias runs through the letters and diaries of nineteenth century New England women and continues to the present day. It is therefore not surprising that several articles address the politics of patronage, exhibition, and economic survival in New England for women artists.

It should be said that this overview is not presented as definitive. It is an exploration from several perspectives of the place of New England women in the larger art world, both past and present, and an introduction to the vitality and promise of women working in the area.

Finally, I would like to thank many people who have been especially helpful to this enterprise: Cynthia Navaretta, who first suggested the project and saw to its completion: Sylvia Moore, Editor; Judy Seigel, Editorial Consultant; Tess Cedarholm, Katherine Dibble, and Sinclair Hitchings of the Boston Public Library, who supported the 1987 Women's Caucus for Art meeting; Susan Greendyke, Art Collections Manager of the Archives of American Art; the librarians of the Schlesinger Library, Radcliffe College, and the Archives of the Wellesley College Library, as well as my own institution, Simmons College; and finally, and especially, Sarah Sutro, president of the Boston WCA, which sustained the project with support and interest.

— **Alicia Faxon**, Project Editor

INTRODUCTION

New England artists enjoy a physical environment nourishing for creativity: woods as lovely as the Barbizon forest, mountains that could tempt Cezanne from Saint-Victoire, skies to enrapture a Constable, clear lakes, powerful rivers, and the famous rockbound coast. The built environment also has its appeal, so much so that New England's barns, covered bridges, lighthouses, and white, steepled churches have become some of America's most compelling visual clichés.

The region's cultural ambiance, too, has fostered the arts, and from New England have emerged some of our greatest thinkers and writers. While the list of literary artists is perhaps more salient, the visual arts have had their share of notables. Among major artists associated with New England by birth or residence are Copley, Stuart, Homer, Sargent, Saint-Gaudens, Hassam, Marin, Hartley, and Wyeth.

But what of New England's women artists? Articles in this collection demonstrate that New England's women have been in the forefront of the "anonymous" needlecraft arts, achieved successful careers in Italy's artist colonies, were influential in the field of art education and as gallery owners, and virtually indispensable as patrons. Yet where is the Emily Dickenson of the visual arts?

True, Nevelson spent some years and O'Keeffe some summers in Maine, but they are hardly New England artists. Harriet Hosmer, Maria Oakey Dewing, Marguerite Zorach, Kay Sage, and Alice Trumbull Mason are among major "minor" artists whose work was taken seriously, but never sufficiently appreciated. These names and a handful of others stand out from the crowd of talented New England women artists who, for all their years of dedication, considered themselves fortunate to have modest sales, participation in group exhibitions, and small, local reputations.

How many of us have heard of Gilbert Stuart's daughter Jane, a portrait artist of some merit, who supported her mother and sisters by doing copies of her late father's more famous works? Or Elizabeth Gardner, wife of William-Adolphe Bouguereau and a well-known painter in Paris, who was born in New Hampshire? Or socially prominent Lilla

Cabot Perry, an admired "American Impressionist" in her day, who is now chiefly remembered for her association with Monet? Such neglected artists emerge from obscurity now and then. From Connecticut there was the miniaturist Ann Hall, who in 1833 became the first woman to hold full membership in the National Academy of Design, and Fidelia Bridges, who specialized in paintings of birds and coastal scenes. Another miniaturist, Sarah Goodridge, opened a studio in Boston in 1820. (Her sister Eliza was an artist.too.) Also from Massachusetts were Ruth Henshaw Bascom, who did pastel portraits in the first half of the nineteenth century, and Gertrude Fiske, winner of many awards in the twenties, who was the first woman appointed to the State Art Commission of Massachusetts. How many other names have never emerged?

In New England, as elsewhere, women patrons played a major role in preserving art for future generations. In addition to Isabella Stuart Gardner and the other Massachusetts and Maine philanthropists described in these pages, there were women like French-born Francine Clark, who first encouraged her husband to collect nineteenth century French art and then founded with him the museum in Williamstown, Massachusetts, that bears their names. Another was Theodate Pope Biddle, who collaborated with Stanford White on the design of a home in Farmington, Connecticut, incorporating her family's art collection. This building eventually became the Hill-Stead Museum.

Many of America's art colonies have a debt to women. In Old Lyme, Connecticut, at the turn of the century, Florence Griswold began a thriving art colony in her boarding house. Matilda Browne and Lydia Longacre were two artists who worked there, along with Childe Hassam and Willard Metcalf. At the start of World War I, a group of women hastily returned from Europe and settled in Provincetown, Massachusetts, that paradigm of summer art colonies. There they made history as "Provincetown Printers," workers in wood-block. Among them were Ethel Mars, Ada Gilmore, Maude Squires, Mildred McMillen, Agnes Weinrich, and Blanche Lazzel. And at the Skowhegan School in Maine, Anne Poor was a teacher and co-director for nearly 15 years, and during her tenure did outdoor frescos on the campus.

There are today encouraging signs of contemporary efforts on behalf of women artists. Museums have presented group shows of women's art, such as the two at the Joan Payson Whitney Gallery in Portland, Maine. We have reprinted an adapted version of the catalog essays for these exhibitions. In New Haven, Connecticut, Ann Langdon founded the feminist Gnosis Gallery, and in Wakefield, Rhode Island, the Hera Cooperative Art Gallery has sponsored exhibitions and cultural programs since 1974. In Northampton, Massachusetts, the Hestia Art Collective painted a mural depicting the history of Northampton. In Hanover, New Hampshire, the A.V.A. Gallery has been supportive of women artists, who comprise over half of those regularly showing at the gallery.

The difficulties women faced were not exclusive to New England: the trivialization of their efforts and aspirations, the barrier to getting an education, the "womanly" duties that limited time for creativity. Class and economics also played a part. Outside of the cities and university towns, culture was often hard to come by. Among working class and farm families there was little time or money to enjoy the arts, though a needlework picture or a portrait of a family member might be framed and admired. It has never been easy for women artists.

In provincial areas, attitudes had scarcely changed as late as the 1940s. At that time I lived in a small New Hampshire town. Not only were the visual arts not taught in my school, but there was never even a visit to the great Orozco frescos at nearby Dartmouth College, much less a class trip to Boston. The visual arts were not esteemed— they were ignored.

Later I studied briefly at the Portland (Maine) School of Art, where I learned about Winslow Homer, but not Georgia O'Keeffe or Mary Cassatt. Years passed before I would be stunned to learn of the wealth of women's art in the world. Sadly, women are still expressing reget for their lack of role models and the discouragement of their aspirations.

This book partly deals with the women artists called "pioneers" by William David Barry, signifying the originators who paved pathways for others to follow. It also includes the "pilgrims" who literally traveled to foreign lands in order to work and live freely in ways New England would not allow, and those who made figurative pilgrimages as devotees of art, despite the hardships of the journey.

We had originally intended to include material from each New England state, but discovered that the lack of activity or research in many areas made this impractical. Many of the articles are written by or about women from the Boston area. This is not only because the city has a rich cultural heritage, but also because there is a resurgence of interest in feminist history among art scholars, educators, and artists in the Boston region today.

The articles fall naturally into two divisions: historic research and descriptive analysis of contemporary work. Our task has been to select and present interesting facets of our topic— what New England women in the visual arts achieved in the past, and what today's New England women artists are doing.

— **Sylvia Moore**, Editor

HERA Women's Cooperative Art Center and Gallery, Wakefield, Rhode Island.

PART ONE

HISTORIC PERSPECTIVES

Anne Whitney, *Charles Sumner*, 1900, Harvard Square, Cambridge.

THE WHITE MARMOREAN FLOCK ―――
――― WOMEN SCULPTORS IN ROME ―――

Surprisingly, one of the first cohesive groups of New England women artists appeared not in New England itself, but in Italy. This was the "white, marmorean flock" (so described by Henry James in his 1903 biography of sculptor William Wetmore Story) who congregated around the American actress Charlotte Cushman (1816-1876) in Rome. This sisterhood of New England women sculptors included **Harriet Hosmer** (1830-1908) from Watertown, Massachusetts; **Louisa Lander** (1826-1923) from Salem; **Emma Stebbins** (1815-1882) of New England lineage (c.1820-1877), born in Dorset, Vermont; **Florence Freeman** (1825-1876) from Boston; **Edmonia Lewis** (c.1834 or 1845- after 1911), who studied sculpture in Boston and sold her first works there; and **Anne Whitney** (1821-1915), also from Watertown. Of these seven, we will look at the career of the four best documented, sculptors whose work can be seen at a number of public sites and collections in New England: Hosmer, Stebbins, Lewis, and Whitney.

Why, in a day when women seldom lived independently of men or even traveled alone, did these women go to Rome to begin their careers? It was because Rome in the neoclassical era, like Paris in the late nineteenth century and New York in the twentieth, was a magnet for sculptors wanting to study seriously and produce great art. Rome, with its many collections of antique sculpture and its classical architecture, was an encyclopedia of forms for the budding neoclassical sculptor. Fine marble was abundant, as were handsome models. There were also skilled Italian craftsmen to help prepare the marble blocks for carving and to do the drudgery of making replicas of successful pieces. The climate was mild and living was inexpensive.

Rome had a flourishing American and British colony of male sculptors, including John Gibson (1790-1866), Thomas Crawford (1813-1857), William Wetmore Story (1819-1895), Richard Saltonstall Greenough (1819-1904), William Henry Rhinehart (1825-1874), Randolph Rogers (1825-1892), Chauncy B. Ives (1810-1894), Augustus Saint-Gaudens (1848-1907), and Benjamin Paul Akers (1825-1861). There were also the important literary figures Robert and Elizabeth Barrrett Browning, close friends of Harriet Hosmer, and Nathaniel Hawthorne, who used

Hosmer and Louisa Lander as models for the women artists in *The Marble Faun,* published in 1860. Thus Rome offered the chance to study with the best sculptors and more freedom and opportunity than New England afforded.

The catalyst for the migration from New England was not a visual artist but a theatrical artist, Charlotte Cushman, who took the budding sculptors under her wing and used her contacts in Rome to further their careers. Harriet Hosmer met Cushman when the actress was on tour in Boston in 1851. As a result, Hosmer traveled with her father to Paris, where they were met by Cushman, arriving in Rome on November 12, 1852.[1]

Harriet Goodhue Hosmer was born in Watertown, Massachusetts, the daughter of a doctor. Because her mother and sister had died early of consumption, her father encouraged the girl to lead an outdoor life: riding, shooting, hunting, swimming, and boating— in short, a prescription for a "tomboy" or an emancipated, independent female. She was sent to a "progressive" institution in Lenox, Mrs. Charles Sedgewick's school, where her independence and talents were encouraged and where she met women who served as role models for a serious career.

Leaving school in 1849, Hosmer began her study with Boston sculptor Paul Stephens. To learn to represent the human body, she applied for courses in anatomy in New England, but was refused admission because she was a woman. In the fall of 1850 she visited her school friend Cornelia Crow in St. Louis, and through the influence of Cornelia's father, Wayman Crow, was admitted to the anatomy class of the St. Louis Medical College

After receiving her diploma she returned to Watertown to start work in her studio, swinging a four-and-one-half pound mallet nearly ten hours a day as she worked marble. Her first important piece was a bust of *Hesper* done 1851-52, now in the Watertown Library. The concept of Hesper, the Evening Star, took its inspiration from Tennyson's 1850 poem, *In Memoriam*;

> "Sad Hesper o'er the buried sun
> And ready, thou, to die with him,

Thou watchest all things ever dim
and dimmer, and a glory done:"

The sculpture, in the prevailing popular neoclassical style of busts of allegorical or mythological women, is a subject which appears to be unique to Hosmer. It is based on antique models suggesting both the sleep of evening and the final sleep of death.

When Hosmer arrived in Rome she began advanced study of sculpture techniques with John Gibson, who had arrived from England in 1817 and had been a pupil of both Canova and Thorvaldsen. Under Gibson's tutelage Hosmer produced marble busts of *Daphne* (Washington University Gallery of Art, St. Louis) and *Medusa* (Private collection) in 1853-54. *Oenone* of c.1854-55 (Washington University Art Gallery) was a complete figure in marble, representing the bride Paris deserted for Helen of Troy. It is likely the subject came from Tennyson's poem *Oenone* rather than from an antique source.

In 1854 Harriet's father, suffering from financial and possibly emotional distress, told his daughter to come home, since he could no longer support the expense of her career. Her response appears in a letter of January 9,1854, to Wayman Crow: "My father has made known to you his ill-fortune and had he made it known to me [earlier] I certainly should have adopted the course I mean to pursue— that of supporting myself."[2] With this end in view she produced in 1856 her most popular sculpture, *Puck on a Toadstool.* The subject was taken from Shakespeare's *A Midsummer Nights' Dream.* Hosmer's version was a chubby elf perched on a toadstool holding a beetle over his head, a charming marble baby so popular that she eventually made fifty replicas. One was in the collection of the Prince of Wales (later King Edward VII). Hosmer created this popular figure knowing it would give her economic independence and finance her more serious work, as she wrote Wayman Crow on March 11, 1858: "Did I tell you I have another for Puck? He has already brought me his weight in silver."[3] Indeed he had, selling first at $500 apiece for the early replicas[4] and eventually at $1,000 each.[5]

In 1856 Crow succeeded in getting Hosmer a commission for *Beatrice Cenci* (Shelley's heroine from the poem, *The Cenci)* for the Mercantile Library in St. Louis. This, probably Hosmer's best known work, was exhibited at the Royal Academy in London in 1857 to great acclaim before being shipped to St. Louis.

Hosmer began a seven-foot marble sculpture of *Zenobia* in 1858. The original is now lost, although a smaller version is in the collection of the Wadsworth Atheneum, Hartford and a replica of the head is in the Watertown Library collection. Zenobia was a Queen of Palmyra, co-ruler with her husband Odenathus, who died in 266 A.D. She continued alone as a successful ruler and extended Palmyra's power until her capture in 272 by the Emperor Aurelian, who destroyed Palmyra and took the queen to Rome in chains. Consulting with her friend, the art historian Anna Jameson (1794-1860), author of *Sacred and Legendary Art* (1848) and *Memoirs of Early Italian Painters* (1854)[6], Hosmer represented Zenobia in classical costume and *contrapposto* pose, walking chained in Aurelian's triumphal procession. Zenobia's expression of sadness and inwardness gives the sculpture a majesty, thoughtfulness, and strength beyond the usual neoclassical renderings. It was shown in 1862 at the International Exhibition in London, and the original was purchased by Alman Griswold of New York. Several replicas were made.

Hosmer's *Zenobia* toured the United States in 1864-65 and was viewed by thousands in New York, Boston, and Chicago, much as Hiram Powers' *Greek Slave* had in 1847-49. It may not be too fanciful to see Zenobia's triumphal tour as an answer to Powers' view of women. Powers showed a life-sized, chained Greek woman, nude, defenseless, and in the process of being sold in a Turkish slave market. This work, modeled on the *Venus de Medici* in the Uffizi Gallery, was an obvious object of male fantasy and desire. Hosmer's *Zenobia* is over life size, a queenly draped figure of a woman who had ruled an empire and governed men. Though in chains, she still wore a crown of state and royal robes. Through her, Hosmer expressed the majesty of women and implied their right to political power in a time when women had few rights.

In 1858, in acknowledgment of her success, Hosmer was made a member of the Roman Academy. This was a high honor, one which vindicated her professionalism to those who laughed at the idea of a woman becoming a sculptor. In 1865 she responded to another challenge, the idea that a woman sculptor could not successfully portray the classsical male nude, in her *Sleeping Faun* (Museum of Fine Arts, Boston). Here she portrays a sensuous, partially draped demigod in repose, a most satisfactory reply to denigrations of female sculptural ability. At the Dublin Exhibition of 1865 it was sold on opening day. Hosmer not only made a number of replicas, but also followed it with a companion piece, *The Waking Faun.*

Hosmer was now well launched and had numerous patrons, many in England where her work was especially appreciated. Her late works included *The African Sybil* of 1889, in which her sympathy with the black race was evident, and *Queen Isabella* of 1891-94, which exalted a female heroine, commissioned by the city of San Francisco.

One of Hosmer's close friends in Rome was Emma Stebbins. Stebbins, born in New York, had begun her artistic career as a painter, but in 1857, at age 42, she moved to Rome to study sculpture. Through Hosmer she met John Gibson, who encouraged her work, and she studied with Benjamin Paul Akers (1825-1861). Her earliest known sculpture was a statuette of Joseph. Stebbins also met Charlotte Cushman, who became a dominant figure in her life and whose biography Stebbins wrote in 1878 after Cushman's death. In 1859 a bust of Charlotte Cushman was commissioned by R.D. Shepherd of Shepherdston, England. The bust was so successful that Stebbins made three replicas.

Stebbins became involved with historical subjects in 1860 when she did a bas relief of *The Treaty of Henry Hudson with the Indians* for the New York collector Marshall O. Roberts. This work evidently gave him confidence in Stebbins' skill, and in 1861 he commissioned a free standing marble sculpture of Columbus, which was finished in 1867. Roberts presented it to the Commissioners of Central Park. It was installed near 102nd Street in New York City; after vicissitudes, it was re-erected in the Brooklyn Civic Center in 1971.[7] Also in 1860 August Heckscher, who had made his money in coal and commerce, commissioned a pair of allegorical marble sculptures, *Industry*, or *The Mine,* and *Commerce* , or *The Sailor*, each 28" high. They are now in the Heckscher Museum, Huntington, New York. These statuettes adapt the classical *contrapposto* pose for figures wearing the dress of their occupations.

Stebbins did her two most important public commissions in bronze. The first stands in front of the State House on Beacon Street and is very familar to Bostonians: a full length statue of Horace Mann (1796-1859), commissioned in 1861 and cast in Munich in 1864. The sculpture was made at the request of Dr. Howe, head of the commission, who was particularly anxious that the representation of Mann, called "the Apostle of Female Education," should be executed by a woman sculptor. Dedicated on July 4,1865, it is an impressive work, showing the education reformer holding a book in his left hand and motioning with his right. His nineteenth century clothing, loathed by neoclassical sculptors, is effectively hidden by a classically draped cloak, and his features, though realistic, have been classicized. There is a solemnity and purpose in the sculpture which displays both Stebbins' formal and expressive powers.

Her other major commission in bronze, much beloved of Central Park strollers, is the *Angel of the Waters* fountain at the Bethesda Pool, commissioned in 1863, and installed in July, 1871. This poetic statue, taken from the gospel of St. John 5: 2-4, shows an angel descending to bless the water for healing and for health. After completing this piece, Stebbins left Rome in 1870 and settled in Newport, Rhode Island, doing little sculpture after that date.

The next sculptor to come to Rome was Edmonia Lewis, in many ways the most original of the group. The beginnings of her life are shrouded in mystery. All sources agree she was the daughter of a Black father and a Chippewa mother, but the dates of her birth are given variously from 1843 to 1846, 1843 being most probable. Similarly, her birthplace is given variously as Greenbush, New York (near Albany); Boston, Massachusetts; Greenhigh, Ohio; and New York City. The case is further complicated because at present there is no Greenhigh in Ohio; no birth records were kept in Ohio before 1867; and neither in the Registry Division of the city of Boston nor in New York City is there any record of her birth.

Lewis was brought up by her mother's family (her Indian name being Wildfire) until, in 1859, she entered Oberlin College in Ohio, the first college to accept women and Black students. She studied at Oberlin until 1862, when she was accused of poisoning two fellow students.

Lewis was acquitted of the charge after a brilliant defense by the Black lawyer, John Mercer Langston, but she left Ohio, arriving in Boston during the summer of 1862 with letters to William Lloyd Garrison (1805-1879) and other Abolitionist leaders. Garrison, learning of her desire to be a sculptor, sent her to Edward Brackett for lessons. She progressed rapidly. Her first works were a medallion of John Brown, the Abolitionist leader of Harper's Ferry, and a plaster bust of Colonel Robert G. Shaw, who died leading the first Black regiment from the North in the Civil War. Lewis created the bust of the hero from photographs. Lydia Maria Child (1802-1880) commented on the work in *The Liberator* of January 20, 1865:

"I confess when she first mentioned her intention of making a bust of Colonel Shaw from photographs, I feared she would make a lamentable failure. But when I went to see the bust in clay, I was very agreeably surprised. I thought the likeness extremely good, and the refined face had a firm yet sad expression as of one given consciously, though willingly, to martyrdom, for the rescue of his country and the redemption of a race."[8]

Edmonia Lewis earned enough money from the sale of replicas of these two works to go to Rome to study. Fittingly, one of the first to welcome and encourage her was Harriet Hosmer, and Lewis became a valued member of the group around Charlotte Cushman. Lewis' first major work in Rome was *Forever Free*, commissioned as a gift to William Lloyd Garrison and completed in marble in 1867. It shows a Black man and woman with their chains breaking, an obvious reference to Lincoln's Emancipation Proclamation and the freeing of the slaves, another example of the way Lewis developed a personal iconography from her Black ancestry to convey her ideas forcefully and expressively.

Around 1870 Lewis did a number of portrait busts and medallions of men important to the abolition of slavery: Abraham Lincoln, Charles Sumner, Wendell Phillips, William Wetmore Story, and Henry Wadsworth Longfellow. Longfellow's bust, modelled in clay in 1869, carved in marble in 1871, and now in the Schlesinger Library at Radcliffe, had special significance for her. The poet had published in 1855 *The Song of Hiawatha* a saga of the Ojibway tribe (the Indian

name for Chippewa), her mother's people. On Longfellow's visit to
Rome in 1869, she followed him around trying to catch a likeness until
his brother brought the poet to sit for her at her studio.[9]

Lewis used characters from *The Song of Hiawatha* for several of her
pieces, the best-known being *The Old Indian Arrowmaker and His
Daughter* of 1872 (National Museum of American Art, Washington,
DC). This sculpture shows Minnehaha, Hiawatha's future bride, sitting
beside her father as Hiawatha first saw her. The poses of the figures are
naturalistic, and the marble is carved with great sensitivity to light and
shade. The difference in the textures of hair, skin, and animal hide is
subtly conveyed, and the work has a presence beyond its narrative
aspects.

Between 1872 and 1876 Lewis created *The Death of Cleopatra*, now
lost. The piece, shown in the Philadelphia Exhibition of 1876, was
highly praised. Lewis depicted the Egyptian ruler not as an Oriental
seductress but as an African woman caught in the agonizing throes of
death. The sculptor sacrified beauty for terror and idealization for
impact and immediacy. By relating Cleopatra to her own African
ancestry, Lewis created a unique image of the dying queen.

In 1875 Lewis represented *Hagar in the Wilderness* in marble, now in
the National Museum of American Art. The subject comes from
Genesis 16:1-6. Lewis' choice of Hagar was unusual if not unique in
nineteenth century sculpture. Hagar was both an Egyptian, a symbol of
the Black woman, and a bondswoman, or slave, as Blacks had been
until recently in America. Lewis was representing in Hagar her own
ancestors, for in this era, Hagar was considered the "mother" of all those
of African descent. Moreover, Lewis said of the sculpture that it
represented a common bond with "all women who have struggled and
suffered"[10] It is this universal quality which makes Lewis' portrayal of
Hagar so moving a work of art. Hagar is shown as a graceful figure
with clasped hands looking upward as she walks. The drapery and hair
are skillfully handled to indicate the forward thrust of the figure, giving
the illusion of motion. The sculpture is less self-contained than earlier
works, appearing to reach out into the spectators' space. Although
Hagar is a victim of Society, she is seen here in a moment of
revelation, receiving a promise from God of a mighty heritage of

descendants.

Lewis made several trips to America but returned to Rome to end her days. The date of her death is unknown. She is now recognized as the first important Black woman sculptor, and an artist of force and originality whose subjects transcended the usual limitations of the neoclassical style.

We know about Lewis's career, not only from her contacts with Harriet Hosmer and Charlotte Cushman, but also through her friendship with the sculptor, Anne Whitney, who came to Rome in 1867. Whitney, like Hosmer, was born in Watertown, Massachusetts. She was the youngest of seven children and grew up in a liberal, Abolitionist family. Unable to marry the man she loved because of the taint of insanity in his family,[11] she turned to teaching in the Salem schools, writing poetry (a book of her poems was published by Appleton Company, New York in 1859) and, in 1855, modeling in clay. Her first known work, in 1859, was a marble bust of a young girl, *Laura Brown* (now in the National Museum of American Art, Washington, DC). She first exhibited at the National Academy of Design in 1860 and was planning to go to Rome for further study when the Civil War broke out. In 1862-63 she created a life-size figure in marble of Lady Godiva (private collection), one of history's first feminist heroines and one who took action for social justice. This was inspired by the 1842 Tennyson poem about Lady Godiva's ride in Coventry covered only by her long hair, to save the people from a crushing tax.

During this time, Whitney studied anatomy with the sculptor and doctor William Rimmer in Boston, and in 1867 she went to Rome to complete her education. One of the first products of her Italian stay was the plaster of *Roma,* in 1869. It was cast in bronze in 1890 and is now on view at the Wellesley College Museum. The sculpture is a brilliant portrayal of an old beggar woman, sitting hunched over like an ancient sibyl, an aged crone whose glories are in memory.

When Whitney returned to Boston in 1873, she received several commissions, the most important being from the Massachusetts Legislature for a marble statue of *Samuel Adams* to represent the state in the Statuary Hall in the U.S. Capitol building. This was so successful that she was commissioned to do a replica in bronze, installed at Faneuil Hall in Boston in 1880. She also sculpted a head of the poet *John Keats*, a bronze for Keats Memorial House in Hampstead, England (the plaster model is in the Watertown Library).

In 1875 Whitney's plaster model of a life-sized seated figure of *Charles Sumner* (model in the Watertown Library) won a contest for a public sculpture of the Abolitionist senator in Boston. When the jury dicovered the winner was a woman, they disqualified her and gave the commission to Thomas Ball. She had her revenge in 1900 when her sculpture was cast in bronze and installed in Harvard Square, Cambridge. Whitney was then eighty years old. Also in 1875, on a trip to Rome, she spent several months studying sculpture in France, which resulted in the bronze head, *Le Modele*, of an old French peasant woman (Museum of Fine Arts, Boston).

One of the main concerns in Whitney's life and work were her Abolitionist sympathies, shown in her poem of October,1850, *The Fugitive Slave Bill*. Her sculptures echoed this theme: her colossal representation of Africa (1863-1864), (now destroyed), Toussaint L'Ouverture (1870), and busts of William Lloyd Garrison (1879), Harriet Beecher Stowe, Lucy Stone (1892, the Boston Public Library), and *Harriet Martineau* (destroyed in a fire in 1914), as well as in her sculpture of *Charles Sumner*. After her return from Rome she received a commission for a bronze sculpture of *Leif Ericsson*, which was cast at Mossman foundry in Chicopee in 1885 and installed on October 29, 1887, on Commonwealth Avenue, Boston, where it stands today.

Letters in Wellesley College library testify to Whitney's friendship with Harriet Hosmer (they addressed each other as "sister"), Emma Stebbins, and Edmonia Lewis, although she did not belong to the Cushman circle when she was in Rome. Like Hosmer, who corresponded with Susan B. Anthony, Anne Whitney wrote to feminists Lucy Stone, Louisa May Alcott, and Lydia Maria Child. All were aware of women artists' struggle for recognition. They believed in living a celibate life, since it was impossible to have a family and a responsible, demanding career in sculpture in a day when marriage usually meant many children and a multitude of domestic responsibilities.

Whitney, who lived to be 93 years old, was famed and respected in her lifetime. Since her death, like many works by "the white, marmorean flock," some of her sculptures have disappeared from public view, either lost, destroyed, or whereabouts unknown. Nevertheless, she was one of the most successful sculptors of public commissions, producing three major works in Boston alone. Another major legacy that Whitney and her independent, creative, and hard-working colleagues left was a history of successful women artists. Their level of achievement and renown was scarcely matched by women for another century.

Location of Works

PUBLIC SITES (*Massachusetts, unless otherwise noted*)
BOSTON
State House, Beacon St., **Emma Stebbins**, *Horace*
Fanueil Hall, **Anne Whitney**, *Samuel Adams*
Commonwealth Ave. Mall, **Anne Whitney**, *Leif Ericsson*
CAMBRIDGE
Harvard Square, **Anne Whitney**,*Charles Sumner*
Mt. Auburn Cemetery, **Edmonia Lewis**, *Hygeia*

MUSEUMS
BOSTON: Museum of Fine Arts, **Harriet Hosmer**, *Sleeping Faun;*
Anne Whitney, *Le Modele*
WELLESLEY: Wellesley College, **Anne Whitney**, *Roma*
AMHERST: Amherst College Museum of Art, **Margaret Foley**,*William Cullen Bryant* (medallion)
BURLINGTON: Robert Hull Fleming Museum of Art, University of Vermont, **Margaret Foley**, *Roman Lady* (medallion)

LIBRARIES
BOSTON: Boston Public Library Rare Books Room, **Harriet Hosmer**, *Clasped Hands of the Brownings;* Boston Public Library Bates Hall, **Anne Whitney**, *Lucy Stone*
CAMBRIDGE: Schlesinger Library, Whitney Room, **Harriet Hosmer**, *Clasped Hands of the Brownings* (plaster); **Edmonia Lewis**, *Longfellow* (bust)
WATERTOWN: Watertown Free Public Library, **Harriet Hosmer**, *Goethe* (medallion); *Hesper* (bust); *Lady ConstanceTalbot* (medallion); *John Gibson* (medallion);*Wayman Crow*, (bust); **Anne Whitney**, *Keats head* (plaster), *Charles Sumner* (plaster); **Margaret Foley**, *Ideal Female Italian Head* (medallion)

WELLESLEY: Wellesley College Library, **Harriet Hosmer,***Clasped Hands of the Brownings;* **Anne Whitney,** *Eben Horseford* (bust)
NORTHAMPTON: Smith College Library, **Anne Whitney,***William Lloyd Garrison* (plaster)
VERGENNES, VT.: Bixby Memorial Free Library, **Margaret Foley,** *Young Trumpeter*

HISTORICAL SOCIETIES
BOSTON: Massachusetts Historical Society, **Anne Whitney,** *William Lloyd Garrison* (bust)

Notes
1. J. Leach, *Bright Particular Star: The Life and Times of Charlotte Cushman*, (New Haven: 1979), p.250.
2. Harriet Hosmer Collection, Schlesinger Library, Radcliffe College, A-162, folder 4, Letter to Wayman Crow, January 9, 1854, 1.
3. Ibid., folder 5, Letter to Wayman Crow, March 11, 1854.
4. Ibid., folder 5, Letter to Wayman Crow, Feb. 15, 1857, 4.
5. M.F. Tharp, *The Literary Sculptors* (Durham, 1965), p.84.
6. S. Waller, "The Artist, the Writer, and the Queen: Hosmer, Jameson, and *Zenobia*," *Woman's Art Journal*, Vol.4, No.1 (1983), p.23.
7. W. Gerdts, Jr., *The White Marmorean Flock: Nineteenth Century American Women Neoclassical Sculptors* , Poughkeepsie: Vassar College Art Gallery, 1972.
8. L.M. Child, *The Liberator*, (Jan. 20, 1865), p.12.
9. Anne Whitney Papers, Wellesley College Archives, Anne Whitney to her family, February, 1869.
10. W. Craven, *Sculpture in America*, (New York, 1968), p.334.
11. E. Payne, "Anne Whitney: Sculptures, Art and Social Justice," *Massachusetts Review,* xii, p.246.

—**Alicia Faxon**

Harriet Hosmer, *Zenobia*, 1862. Courtesy Wadsworth Atheneum, Hartford.

Edmonia Lewis, *Hagar*, 1875, National Museum of American Art, Smithsonian Institution, Washington, DC

NEEDLEWORK AS AN EARLY
NEW ENGLAND ART FORM

"With cheerful mind we yield to men
The higher honours of the pen
The needle's our great care,
In this we chiefly wish to shine
How far this art's already mine
This sampler does declare." [1]

The sentiments expressed by eight-year-old Ann Wood in her 1817 sampler verse reflected the creative aspirations of many nineteenth century schoolgirls. Following the standards set for "appropriate" female education and artistic expression, girls continued in the newly organized academies to develop their abilities in the ornamental arts, particularly the art of the sampler or needlework picture. Like generations of women before them, they worked to perfect their skills in the "gentle feminine art" of needlework for a number of reasons. Through the creation of the basic sampler, for example, girls learned skills necessary for making and embellishing household linens. These utilitarian pieces also reinforced lessons that developed basic reading and mathematical skills.

Later in a girl's education, after the basic stitches had been mastered, a final "graduation piece" was undertaken, usually an elaborately detailed needlework picture. These decorative pieces displayed an individual's proficiency with needle and thread, an important asset for "accomplished" young women of the upper classes. Part of the motivation behind the needlework endeavors of nineteenth century women was the sexual lure it provided in the courtship game:

"As she was busily engaged with her needle, she presented a demure, enticing female figure. Indeed, the postures and attitudes of fine sewing exemplified the ideal woman — relaxed and at leisure, posturing prettily, her hands dutifully occupied, showing her industry. She needed to be busy so as not to appear too eager." [2]

An equally important motivating force for the creation of needlework, however, stemmed from the traditional value attached to this ornamental art. As her grandmother's and mother's needlework had been preserved and revered (often included in itemized inventories and wills), so too the daughter's work was treated as valuable, and it was usually professionally framed and hung on a prominent parlor wall. The sewing process offered additional benefits in the realms of socialization (when working with others) and reflection (when working alone). For the creative woman, needlework was an acceptable outlet in the exploration of color, texture, shading, and, occasionally, composition.

Inspiration for the majority of needlework projects undertaken in early nineteenth century female schools, however, was drawn from illustrations and engravings, not from individual imagination. Originality of design was not encouraged, since educators were more concerned with ability to display patience and proficiency in technique. Students in New England academies had the opportunity to choose subjects from engraving collections owned by their schools, which often listed their print and illustration holdings in advertisments. Prospective students and their parents were invited to view these collections in advance as a means of choosing the most appropriate academic environment, which indicates the importance of needlework in the academy experience. Among subjects most frequently chosen by students were pastoral settings of the British countryside, scenes from classical mythology, Shakespearean subjects, and occasionally historical subjects. Religious subjects were rare in this period, except for mourning art, sentimental pieces created as memorials to family members or patriotic leaders.

Scenes chosen by the adolescent needleworkers were for the most part intended to illustrate a sublime moral idea or dramatic moment.[3] Romance, sentimentality, nostalgia, and drama were factors in the choice. Several of the engravings identified as sources for student work were done by British engraver Thomas Burke. Burke was one of the chief interpreters of Angelica Kauffman's work, as was Francesco Bartolozzi, another engraver known as a source of schoolgirls' subjects. Both were involved in an ambitious project published in 1805 by John and Josiah Boydell, *The Shakespeare Gallery*, which illustrated scenes from all the Shakespearean plays. Quite possibly the Boydell catalogue was part of the New England academy portfolio holdings.

Typically, once the subject had been chosen, American needlework pieces were prepared for work through a series of precise steps. The design was first transferred to the silk. Once the fabric had been marked, a backing fabric, usually coarse, durable linen, would be attached to the silk by a simple basting stitch around the outside edge (on smaller pieces, merely reinforcing the edges with backing fabric sufficed). Finally, the double layered fabric was tacked to a wooden frame. In working with silk, the necessity of a smooth, even surface in creating an expertly finished piece required a wooden embroidery frame, which, combined with the linen backing fabric, kept the silken surface taut.

Individuality, or the creative expression of the needleworker, came into play once she began to choose colors and stitches. Because female students in the academies tended to come from wealthy families, their materials included imported threads (chenille, raw silk, and gold), offering a wider range of colors and textures than that of their less affluent peers. More complicated stitches, in addition to those mastered in each girl's basic sampler, were incorporated to enrich and differentiate surface detail. Water, for example, was often suggested by a series of long/short stitches carefully placed to allow the silk fabric underneath to show through, suggesting the shimmering quality of the water's surface. Foliage areas were worked with ornamental stitches to recreate the rich tapestry of various bushes and trees. Tiny seed stitches haphazardly placed could effectively suggest , for example, the motion and life of a bush caught by a sudden gust of wind, while long/short stitches laid compactly side by side with a boundary of outline stitch could suggest a substantial leafy configuration. The most frequently used stitch in the finished academy project was long/short, basic "brush stroke" of the needlework picture, which could be effective in figure modelling and landscape detail alike. Rounded torso and architectural structures emerged through the careful placement of the long/short stitch. With one stitch placed beside another in a staggered fashion, long/short could be used to fill large areas in a light, "feathered" way, allowing colors to blend and subtle linear detail to be defined.

One particularly masterful example of nineteenth century schoolgirl needlework is a piece entitled *Cymbeline*, done by Ann Trask in 1812. Worked almost entirely in long/short stitch, it embodies the high standards exacted by Trask's teacher, Susanna Rowson. Thought has been given to the careful placement of each stitch, so the finished work is smooth and even. In silk embroidery, direction of the stitches is extremely important, and Trask's awareness of that fact is apparent in her expert handling of figure modelling, architectural detail, and fabric depiction. The only awkwardness is in the stance of the palace guard on the right — his feet and legs are not quite convincingly placed. But on the whole Trask has admirably duplicated the Thomas Burke engraving which inspired the work.

Her choice of subject was in keeping with tradition. The moment depicted is when Imogen, the king's daughter, defies the wishes of her parents and marries "a poor but worthy gentleman." It is only a tiny part of the romantic text, occurring early in Act 1, but obviously represents an independent act that ignited the imagination of the young needleworker. It is from this dramatic moment that the entire story unfolds. Perhaps for Trask it represented a type of personal freedom she dreamed of for herself: independence within a romantic framework.

Trask's technical skill is clearly revealed in viewing the back side of the work. Each thread has been carefully woven into the fabric (as opposed to using knots to anchor a new thread), making the back almost as even and finished as the front. The back also provides an opportunity to see the colors as originally chosen and worked, unaffected by the wear and discoloration of time. Trask's palette emphasized the regal tone of the piece with rich blues, reds, and golds predominating. The distribution and balance of color demonstrates an understanding of color principles as sophisticated as her needlework skills.

Painted detail in *Cymbeline*, specifically facial detail, helps date the piece. As enthusiam for needlework began to wane in the early nineteenth century, and women began to look for short cuts in completing their projects, painted detail increased. Skies, water, and facial representation were the most commonly painted aspects. While most schools chose to apply watercolor pigment directly to the silk fabric upon completion of the needlework, as in Trask's piece, other options were also available. Occasionally, for example, faces were painted on paper and then either adhered directly to the silk or sandwiched between the silk and a piece of sheer cover fabric. For the most industrious needleworkers, the option of embroidering facial detail also existed. Exactly who was responsible for the painted detail is not clear; possibilities include itinerant artists traveling from school to school, academy instructors, or perhaps the student herself.

As the academies grew in popularity and size, curriculums were expanded to include drawing and painting, French, music, and dancing. The inclusion of drawing and painting classes in the academy program at this time was seen as being "serviceable" to students in needlework[4] by teaching techniques in shading, design, and color more effectively. An early example of a student watercolor done between 1807 and 1809 supports this premise.

The painting of Susanna Rowson's Washington Street establishment strikes one by its similarity to needlework examples of the time. Trees are chenille-like in interpretation and shading, for example, suggesting that the piece may have been a study for a needlework project. Ink outlines around buildings, fences, and foliage could have been easily transferable to silk for adaptation in thread. Even the shading of the curved roof of the main building suggests long/short stitch. A charmingly primitive rendition of the Boston academy, the painting is done with the same precision and painstaking care for which Rowson needlework examples are known. Colors chosen by the young artist, brick red, gold, and forest green, are in keeping with the palette of thread colors often chosen for needlework projects of the time. Whether or not the Rowson painting was intended to become needlework is unknown, but the influence of the artist's experience with needlework in approaching her painting is undeniable.

One of the most popular forms of needlework art for students, and potentially the most creative in terms of composition, was mourning art. Inspired originally in 1799 by an outpouring of national sentiment at the death of George Washington, the art form gradually evolved into more individualized grief therapy created for deceased family members. Several components typifed this ornamental art form; use of silk or satin for the background material, incorporation of hair from the deceased in working the design, hand-painted areas in addition to the silk embroidered segments, and compositional components including an urn, a weeping willow, a tomb, and at least one grieving female figure dressed in classical garb. The overall tone of the piece was always extremely sentimental. It was this aspect that made the form especially appealing to adolescents, who in turn reflected a larger spectrum of feminine emotionalism emerging from the religious atmosphere of the period, the so-called Second Great Awakening. During this period, when the clergy aligned themselves with women in society (or at least the more pious element), emotions were recognized as an appropriate part of religion. Mourning and grief were seen as bringing one closer to God.

An additional influence on the style of mourning art was the revival of the classical style, reflected in the costuming of the figures and the architectural details of the funerary monuments. While overall design requirements for mourning art dictated that the appropriate symbols be included, there was leeway in placement. As the art became more individualized, the needleworker was more active in placement and specific details. A student might, for example, choose to include all her family members in the picture, and the monument depicted might be a rendering of the family tomb. As mourning art evolved, painted figure details and landscape areas significantly increased, reflecting in part the waning enthusiasm for needlework and perhaps an increasing interest in the use of brush and paint as a vehicle for artistic expression. One area in particular, the sky, offered oportunity for painterly exploration. While in some pieces it is merely a wash of color, even and non-dramatic, in others it effectively reflects the emotional tone of the piece, utilizing color and irregular cloud configurations to suggest the turmoil and grief which inspired the work. Students in drawing and painting classes might well have been responsible for the painted surfaces in their pictures in addition to the stitched areas.

What the academy environment offered to the creative female student in the nineteenth century was a supportive learning experience where individual interpretation was encouraged and valued. Students learned about the art of both past and present as they examined portfolios of engravings for their "graduation" needlework pieces. They were taught the artistic techniques of shading, perspective, composition, figure drawing, and landscape and architectural depiction as they sat, needle in hand, working to recreate the engraving before them. They received instruction in color principles and texture considerations as they worked with the silken threads that gave life to their pieces. Finally, they were given the opportunity to study painting and drawing and, as a result, to be involved in the creation of the compositions they "painted" with needle and thread. The pieces they labored over were special in that they were not "functional" in the sense that their mother's and grandmother's needlework had been.. Their stitches had a more lofty purpose than merely to embellish bed linens and children's clothing. The finished work was matted, framed, and hung where family and visitors could appreciate it. Nineteenth century needlework art was valued for the beauty it brought to the room where it was displayed. Through her needlework a student could find a path to creative potential, and through the academy system she could receive the training and support to develop it.

Notes:
1. Anna Sebba, Samplers — *Five Centuries of Gentle Craft* (New York: Thames & Hudson, Inc., 1975), p.3
2. Susan Burrows Swan, *Plain and Fancy — American Women and their Needlework 1700-1850* (New York: Holt, Rinehart & Winston, 1977), p.79.
3. Jane C. Nylander, "Some Print Sources of New England Schoolgirl Art," *Antiques* (August 1976), p.296.
4. Swan, p.69.

BIBLIOGRAPHY
1. Harbeson, Georgiana Brown. *American Needlework.* (New York: Coward McCann, Inc., 1938).
2. Nylander, Jane C. "Evidence of Accomplishment: New England Schoolgirl Art in the Nineteenth Century." catalogue of an exhibition at Old Sturbridge Village, March 20-September 15, 1977. (Old Sturbridge, Inc., 1978).
3. Nylander, Jane C. "Some Print Sources of New England Schoolgirl Art." *Antiques,* (August 1976), pp. 292-302,
4. Swan, Susan Burrows. *American Needlework.* (New York: Crown Publishers. Inc., 1976).
5. Swan, Susan Burrows. *Plain and Fancy: American Women and their Needlework 1700-1850.* (New York: Holt, Rinehart & Winston, 1977).

—Penny Redfield

Unknown, *Mrs. Rowson's School*, 1807-1809. Courtesy of The Bostonian Society.

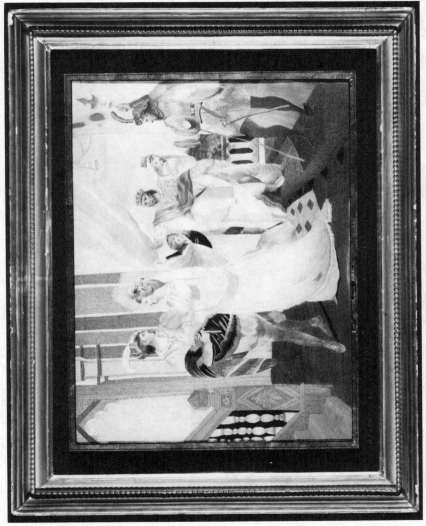

Ann Trask, *Cymbeline*, 1812, Old Sturbridge Village, Massachusetts

John Singer Sargent,
*Isabella Stewart
Gardner*, Gardner
Museum, Boston.

THE GREAT COLLECTORS
ISABELLA STEWART GARDNER AND HER SISTERS

Of the three great painting collections in the Boston area, two are named for women: **Isabella Stewart Gardner**, whose spectacular collection of old master paintings is housed in her own palace-museum, and **Maria Antoinette Evans**, who gave the Museum of Fine Arts such treasures as Vigée-LeBrun's *Portrait of a Young Woman* and Jordaen's *Man and Wife* and a magnificent wing to house them. These are but two of many important women collectors in New England who began accumulating art furnishings for their homes and as a civilizing gesture — to turn raw money into a refined expression of taste. Many of these women supported artists of their own eras, or resurrected schools and styles of art seemingly forgotten. Their emphasis on the arts as a means of bettering society, evident in the founding charters of the museums and art schools they ultimately supported, gave them an aesthetic and altruistic goal.

The most famous art collector of New England was and is Isabella Stewart Gardner, who assembled one of the most stunning groups of paintings and decorative arts in America. Her first passion was rare books and manuscripts, but she soon purchased French landscapes and eighteenth century funishings. When her father died in 1891, leaving her a sizeable inheritance, she began to purchase old master paintings. Working with Harvard-trained art historian Bernard Berenson, who acted as her scout, she planned a comprehensive collection of European art. But her love of Italy prevailed. When her museum opened in 1903, it was her fantasy of a Venetian palace, crowded with masterpieces which included paintings by Piero della Francesca and Botticelli, Titian and Raphael, Rembrandt and Vermeer.

Mrs. Gardner's achievements are well known, but the collecting activities of her Boston peers have been little studied. Because these collections were not enshrined in a private museum or donated *en masse* to a public institution, they are more difficult to reconstruct. Among active collectors were **Sarah Wyman Whitman**, who supplied the funds for the Museum of Fine Arts to purchase Velasquez' portrait of Phillip IV, and the Barna da Siena *Mystical Marriage of Saint Catherine;* **Lilla Cabot Perry**, whose tireless efforts on behalf of Claude Monet made him one of the most popular artists in Boston;

Grace Edwards and her sister **Hannah Marcy**, who bought 57 Impressionist pictures between 1907 and 1924; and Maria Anoinette Evans, who gave one million dollars in memory of her husband for the Museum's painting wing and donated 50 paintings in 1917. Among the most interesting of these turn-of-the-century collectors are **Sarah Choate Sears** and **Susan Cornelia Warren**.

Unlike Isabella Stewart Gardner, whose interest in contemporary art was sporadic and dictated by her personal friendships, Sarah Sears was committed to the patronage of living artists. In 1877, at the age of 19, Sarah Choate married Joshua Montgomery Sears, a real estate magnate and Boston's richest citizen. She studied at the Cowles Art School with Dennis Bunker, and from 1889 to1891 was enrolled at the School of the Museum of Fine Arts. One of her early purchases was a painting by Edmund Tarbell, then the chief instuctor at the School. This brilliant outdoor composition, *Three sisters: A Study in June Sunlight* (Milwaukee Art Center), was first exhibited at the St. Botolph Club in 1891; it was already owned by Mrs. Sears. The same year, she purchased Abbot Thayer's *Virgin Enthroned* (National Museum of American Art) for $8000, the highest price Thayer had ever received, and commissioned him to paint her daughter Helen (Toledo Museum of American Art); three years later she asked Sargent for a second portrait of her daughter (Museum of Fine Arts, Boston). About 1897, she began to collect the work of a little-known painter with an independent approach, Maurice Prendergast. Sarah Sears eventually owned at least ten Prendergasts (watercolors and monotypes) and funded the artist's 1898 trip to Europe. This was a strong show of support for a painter who seldom exhibited at major Boston institutions during his lifetime and did not receive serious critical attention until 1924, when a memorial tribute was written by modern art collector Duncan Phillips.

A founder of the Boston Society of Arts and Crafts, the first such group in America, Mrs. Sears began to make photographs around 1892. She soon came into contact with F. Holland Day, a local pictorialist photographer and publisher. She schemed with Day to establish Boston as a center for pictorialism, and convinced the trustees of the Museum of Fine Arts to allow the use of their galleries as an exhibition center. But they never received the support of Alfred Stieglitz, and the project fell through.[1] Later Mrs. Sears lent her financial support to Stieglitz and his artists at "291," purchasing watercolors by John Marin and Charles Demuth.

Through her friendship with Mary Cassatt, Sarah Sears was drawn to the work of the French Impressionists. About 1905, she bought one of the first paintings by Edouard Manet to enter a Boston collection, *The Street Singer*. She owned two works by Degas, and while it has been published that she purchased Edgar Dégas's *Danseuses à la Barre* in 1912 and presented it to the Louvre, in fact she was outbid by another active woman collector, Mrs. **H.O. Havemeyer**.[2] An active participant in contemporary art movements in Boston, Mrs. Sears also donated scholarship money to local art students. She died in 1935.

Susan Cornelia Warren assembled one of the largest collections in Boston, and was Mrs. Gardner's occasional rival for choice paintings on the market. She had intended to purchase Titian's *Rape of Europa* when it became available from the eighth Earl of Darnley in 1896 and made an offer for the picture upon the advice of Bernard Berenson. But that scholar's first loyalty was to Mrs. Gardner, and when their scheme to purchase Gainsborough's *Blue Boy* fell through, Berenson convinced Gardner to cable her bid on the Titian, thus beating Warren to the ownership of one of the greatest Italian paintings in America.

Mrs. Warren had not begun to collect until somewhat late in her life. The daughter of a Congregational minister of modest means, she married Samuel Dennis Warren in 1847. Warren became extremely wealthy as the founder of Cumberland Mills, a Maine paper manufactory. Susan Warren's first purchases date from the early 1870s, and she continued to collect for 25 years. Like many of her contemporaries, she made her first acquisitions to furnish and embellish her home — decorative objects including china, glass, lacquer, textiles, jewelry, and furniture — but soon grew far beyond household needs. This eclectic and encyclopedic collection, favoring the eighteenth century, paralleled local taste. But her selection of paintings was more varied and guided by her own instincts. As her daughter Cornelia recalled in a written memorial of 1908: "Another and better known instance of my mother's self-training was her collection of paintings. Her taste for porcelain, bronzes, and bric-à-brac had given way to the greater passion for pictures. My father encouraged her to make purchases as opportunity served."

Mrs. Warren bought over 100 paintings, and, like many Bostonians, she favored the Barbizon School. Included were at least six Corots, four Daubignys, three Rousseaus, and five Millets, including *Young Shepherdess,* one of Millet's most monumental and heroic figurative works. The Warrens acquired it through the Paris dealer Durand Ruel from the 1875 sale of the artist's studio. They kept it for only two years, donating it to the Boston Museum in 1877. Other figurative works of the Barbizon School included Corot's *Portrait of a Man* and Couture's *Madame Couture* (now in the Museum of Fine Arts, Boston), both purchased through the Vose Galleries, where Mrs. Warren spent over $20,000 in a single year.[3] American paintings in the Barbizon style also found their place in the Warren collection; including canvases by J. Foxcroft Cole, William Morris Hunt, George Fuller, George Inness, and John LaFarge. Yet purchases such as these were characteristic of the pattern of local collecting in which poetic, light-filled landscapes were objects of choice. Impressive as they are, it is not these paintings which make her collection distinct from others in Boston; rather it is a select group of very different pictures which sets Mrs. Warren apart as a connoisseur.

Some of these were French as well, most notably Jean Leon Gerôme's *L'Eminence Grise* , purchased in 1889. It was the first major painting by this admired French academician to enter a Boston collection.[4] Three works by Delacroix, a Géricault, an Ingres portrait, two oils by Puvis de Chavannes, and a Daumier entitled *The Prison Choir* rounded out her nineteenth century French paintings. Spain was represented by a Goya portrait, and among the English paintings (which Mrs. Gardner ignored after her failure to acquire the *Blue Boy*) were Sir Thomas Lawrence's portraits of Lord and Lady Lyndhurst, the son and daughter-in-law of American painter, John Singleton Copley.

The most outstanding painting in Warren's collection was neither French nor nineteenth century. It was a Renaissance tondo of the Holy Family with Saint Margaret and John by the Florentine painter Filippino Lippi. Now in the Cleveland Museum of Art, the panel was purchased by Mrs. Warren in 1898 after it had been brought to her attention by Berenson, who kept in contact with her son, Edward, a collector of Greek antiquities. With its jewel-like colors, large size, and harmonious treatment of the circular format, it is still considered one of the finest example of Lippi's work in America. The tondo joined several other old masters in the Warren Collection, including works ascribed to Jan Brueghel, Vincenzo Catena, Pieter de Hooch, Hans Memling, Aert van der Neer, Peter Paul Rubens, and Michael Wohlgemuth.

When the noted art critic Charles Caffin attempted to characterize Mrs. Warren's collection in 1903, he wrote: "It bears little or no evidence of having been systematically compiled, but would seem to be rather the product of independent preferences, guided by a cultivated instinct."[5] The bulk of the collection, both painting and decorative arts, was sold at auction in 1902 and 1903.

While the taste for old master paintings continued into the twentieth century, their increasing scarcity and cost made them inaccessible to all but the very wealthy. Nurtured by the cultural nationalism engendered by World War I, many collectors such as Electra Havemeyer Webb, who founded Vermont's Shelburne Museum, began to turn their attention to the arts of America. One of the largest of these groups is the Karolik collection, now in the Boston Museum.

Composed of three distinct parts — eighteenth-century arts, mid-nineteenth century paintings, and works on paper — the Karolik collection has been strongly identified with the flamboyant personality of Russian emigré Maxim Karolik, But the concept of the collection and the source of a great number of the objects was his wife, **Martha Codman Karolik**. Born in 1858 to one of Boston's oldest families, Martha Codman developed a love of art and antiques that was motivated by family pride. In the early 1900s she became interested in acquiring (mostly from other family members) ancestral artifacts, and for her these included portraits of the Codmans and Amorys by John Singleton Copley and Gilbert Stuart, as well as the furnishings and decorative objects associated with the Derby family of Salem and their mansion, Oak Hill. By 1921, Martha Codman had agreed to donate these objects to the Boston Museum; it would become the heart of the first Karolik collection. She met Maxim Karolik in 1927 and instilled in him her love of American Art. They married the following year and together planned to expand her largely Salem and Boston collection by purchasing items from other parts of the country, making of it a three-dimensional textbook of eighteenth-century American design. It opened to the public in 1941, an embodiment of Martha Codman Karolik's taste. Two years later she expressed her enthusiasm for the second collection, to consist of paintings by the forgotten American artists of 1815 to1865. Gathered largely by her husband, this collection was completed and given to the museum one month before Mrs. Karolik's death in 1948.[6]

The decorative arts of the first Karolik collection are superbly crafted examples of the high style. A parallel tradition of vernacular objects became the focus of another impressive collection formed by a New England woman, **Nina Fletcher Little**. Like that of Mrs. Warren, Mrs. Little's collection began as a way to furnish her early eighteenth century home. High style funiture brought high style prices, and Mrs. Little turned toward simpler country designs and related decorative arts. Guided by an article in the newly founded magazine *Antiques*, she made her first purchase, a blue English Staffordshire plate, in 1927. Furniture, clocks, utensils, glass, textiles, and paintings soon followed, and the collection outgrew its original purpose, becoming remarkable for size, variety, and scope.

Despite its enormous scale, the Little collection is marked by careful thought, consideration, and humor. Anonymous provincial artists, whose works combine brilliant color and fanciful design, enjoy equal standing with the most famous of American folk painters. Featured painters include Ammi Phillips, whose widely varied works have only recently been studied, Rufus Hathaway, an itinerant portrait painter and decorative artist who was the subject of a major study by Mrs. Little, and Michele Corne, an Italian-born painter who worked for many wealthy partrons including the Derby family of Salem. Recording all the known facts about the creation and provenance of every object, Mrs. Little has become a connoisseur and scholar of American folk art and decoration.

The tradition of New England women as collectors continues to the present day. Among them are **Lois Torf**, whose enormous collection of prints, over a thousand images, began in 1961 with a Japanese woodcut and now spans the major movements of the twentieth century, and Lois Foster, who with her husband Henry has devoted herself to modern color-field painting and has donated a gallery to the Museum of Fine Arts for its display. As with their predecessors, the major committment of these women is to quality. None of these collections is unified by style, by subject matter, or by the sex of the artist. Instead, they are the manifestation of a passion to own the best.

Notes.
1. Information on Sarah Choate Sears can be found in Estelle Jussim, *Slave to Beauty* (Boston: David R. Godine, 1981), and in Stephanie Mary Buck, *Sarah Choate Sears: Artist, Photographer, and Art Patron*, MFA Thesis (Syracuse University, 1985).
2. The incorrect information appeared in contemporary newspapers (such as the *Boston Transcript*, 18 December 1912) in Buck's thesis, and in Gerald Reitlinger, *The Economics of Taste* (New York: Holt, Rinehart &Winston,1961).
3. Carol Troyen, *The Boston Tradition* (New York: The American Federation of Arts,1980) p.34.
4. Alexandra R. Murphy, "French Paintings in Boston: 1800-1900," *Corot to Braque* (Boston: Museum of Fine Arts, 1979) p. xlvi.
5. Introduction to sale catalogue, *The Collection of the Late S.D. Warren* (New York: American Art Galleries, 1903).
6. Further information on Martha Codman Karolik provided by Cynthia Dunn Fleming, who has work in progress on Mrs. Karolik and her collection.

—**Erica Hirshler**

Emma Stebbins, *Horace Mann*, 1864, State House, Boston. Reproduced through the courtesy of the Commonwealth of Massachusetts, Massachusetts Art Commission.

THE ART EDUCATION OF
WORKING WOMEN 1873-1903

Massachusetts Normal Art School, founded by the state in 1873, revolutionized *who* could study art in this country. As a normal school, it was one of the institutions created as part of a movement to improve the quality of teachers, but as a normal *art* school, it was unique in this county. At that time many people associated art with affluence and privilege. At this fledgling school, art was reinterpreted as the legitimate domain of working people. Descendants reminisce fondly even today about how the school opened the world of art to the whole family because a great aunt, grandmother, or uncle could study there free. Moreover, Massachusetts Normal Art School (henceforth MNAS) and its first director, Walter Smith, transformed not only individuals and families, but also the direction of opportunities in America.

One consequence of the founding of this public art school (now the Massachusetts College of Art), was the creation of a framework in which women developed skills that enabled them to pursue careers in art. Women were central to the plan. Smith wrote:

"There is an unworked mine of untold wealth among us in the art education of women. In the field of general education here I am informed that nine tenths of the teachers are women; and some explanation of its excellence may be found in that fact"[1]

"It seems to me that an infinite amount of good would be done by opening up the whole field of art instruction and art workmanship to the gentler sex. I do hope there shall be absolutely no distinction made concerning the eligibility or disqualification of sex in the students. It is only fair and honest that both should have identically the same training and the same opportunities for becoming 'valuable persons' ...And then we shall attain to one great result...we shall double the agency and area of art culture, and provide employment for a large number of excellent persons who suffer the lack of it now."[2]

Demographics

The enrollment statistics of the MNAS are stunning. Of a total of 117 men and women who received certificates for at least one art specialty in the first thirty years of the school, only 219 were men, while *898* were women.

Learning to draw was for the nineteenth century what computers are to us now. Art teachers were in demand to bring art skills to every home. This demand justified the importation of Walter Smith to Boston by the city and the state jointly, because the powers-that-be perceived the need that Smith articulated in 1872:

"Above all, there is an immediate and pressing need for the creation of a class of public art instructors; for I do not spend a week without receiving requests from different parts of the State of Massachusetts, and from other states as well . . . on the other hand, I have been consulted by many individuals. . . who want to become teachers of art, and to be put into the way of getting the necessary professional instruction. Here then, face to face, are the actual need of the community, and the people who are anxious to minister to that need.[3]

Why were women so important to the scheme of this new school? Since women had proven themselves successful as classroom teachers, it was assumed they would also excel in the teaching of art. A woman whose name comes down to us only as Miss R.L. Hoyt, a student from MNAS' first graduating class who remained as a MNAS faculty member for 38 years, recalled how Walter Smith set out to make his experiment succeed. For the school's first class, Smith recruited as students, artists who already had been teaching drawing in their own studios in Boston. They agreed to enter the first class of the school as pupils in order to ensure good work at the end of the year. He enlisted the sympathies of artists by saying, "Won't you join us, and work with us, for the establishment of this needed school?" Miss Hoyt, who listed herself as one seduced by Smith's plan, recalled, "It was ever difficult to say 'no' to Walter Smith; I replied that I had no plans for the coming year and I would gladly become a member of the school."[4] By saying "member" rather than "student," Hoyt's discomfort with the arrangement showed. That was resolved by the second year, when she became a faculty member. Mercy A. Bailey, Annie E. Blake, Louise M. Field, and N. Dranga all similarly came as students and remained as faculty. Smith thus solved two problems at once: he disguised skilled artists as students so they would produce impressive art work to remove any doubts of those who judged the validity of the school, and, at the same time, he gathered together artists who could be his faculty, for it was not easy to assemble one, particularly to teach along the lines of *his* system.

Because the booming interest in learning to draw continued, each class of MNAS alumni, a huge proportion of whom were women, continued to meet the demand for teachers. The MNAS 1903 Thirtieth Year Circular and Catalogue supplies some details of career paths of the first 30 years' alumni. Since viewers from all the states had sung praises for the display of MNAS student art work at the 1876 Centennial Exhibition in Philadelphia; over the next quarter century MNAS alumni became prized everywhere. Beyond those five who chose to teach at the school that trained them, other women went to various parts of the state of Massachusetts, teaching at normal schools in Bridgewater, Westfield, and Worcester. Some women taught in New York State, at Teachers College, Columbia, and Pratt Institute. Others went further, to the Agricultural College in Manhattan, Kansas, the State Normal University in Illinois, Hampton Institute in Virginia, and St. Louis Normal School in Missouri.

Regardless of whether they had studied specifically to be teachers, many of the alumni taught. Though all but four of the 76 alumni who completed the program "Pedagogy and Supervision" in those first 30 years were women, almost double that number of women entered public school art teaching, a field which burgeoned after Massachusetts' passing of the 1870 Drawing Act, requiring that free drawing classes be offered in every city and town with population in excess of ten thousand. By the turn of the century, 121 (12 percent) of the women graduates had committed themselves to careers as artists teaching and supervising this new subject, art, in classrooms of children from kindergarten through high school.

Art as Technical Education

But why should this modest achievement have gained the school such national prominence? At the time when MNAS was founded, education was in the midst of massive change. The instigator, Horace Mann, Secretary to the Board of Education in Massachusetts, worried about the average working class child trapped in debilitated schools with regressive or nonexistent teaching methods. The education that children received compared adversely with the advance methods he and his wife, educator Mary Peabody Mann, observed in their research tours throughout Europe. Mann captured the public imagination when he returned to the United States and pursued his quest for educational reform that included the teaching of drawing.

Mann's efforts to improve the education of children and adolescents was supported, in 1862, by the federal Morrill Land Grant legislation, which instituted practical studies in public higher education.' With this innovation, agricultural colleges, technological institutes, and MNAS were forged into an unofficial league of kindred institutions, all of which aimed to build a skilled, productive class of people whose learning could be useful and profitable.

Walter Smith, who always thought of education in terms of systems, familiarized himself enough with the educational changes in this country to align his efforts with the movement of the technical institutes and Land Grant colleges. He wrote:

"I have no doubt that eventually, whilst the bond of common tongue, the interests of trade, and the facilities of intercommunication, will forever unite the sovereign states of America into one nation, there will yet be independent departments of science and art in every metropolitan city, from which will emanate the art education of each state. But just as . . . Harvard and Yale . . . may be said to be the national universities of America, so I believe it will be found, that in one or two intellectual centres, there will arise national schools of design, which will be to industrial education, what Harvard and Yale have been to professional education. *Technical education in art and science may be described as the liberal education of the working classes* (my italics) who have not found a home in the universities. . .The evidence is strongly in favor of Boston being the first city in the union to establish a national school of design. . . . (Here he speaks of the school he was in the midst of creating: MNAS). The establishment of a museum of Fine and Industrial Arts in Boston, now in the process of construction, has committed the city to a project which forms an important part of any national system of art education.... A museum, however rich in its contents and perfect in its arrangements for exhibitions, is but a show, unless it combines with its wealth of art the active educational agencies in the classroom which are to transmute its wealth into currency."[5]

For Smith and other masterminds of Boston's artistic development, the museum was an extension of his art school. He wrote of evening lectures in its public lecture hall that would have two-thirds of the seats offered free to working men and women and the remaining third to art students, where all would be engaged in listening, taking notes, or drawing in their sketchbooks.[6] The museum was to be the laboratory for MNAS' technical education.

Redefinition of Work

The opening of this public art school in 1873 was the result of substantial crises besetting the nation. Art was a subject that Americans had been concerned with before the Civil War, but after the war, art truly became an obsession.

The Civil War had left broken families, drained of spirit and resources, and maimed the nation with a huge debt. Massachusetts was particularly worried because, though it had been in the forefront of industrial production with its vast mills in Lowell and Lawrence, other states were rapidly gaining the technology that had been its advantage. Something had to be done to guarantee to Massachusetts the industrial preeminence to which it had become accustomed.

As if competition between the states was not enough, other threats came from abroad. Steam transportation now could deliver foreign-made products anywhere, and as these rival products arrived in ever greater numbers, the fine workmanship displayed in them aroused curiosity and envy. When the people who made the fascinating products also arrived, Massachusetts could waste no time before doing something to hold her own in the competition.

Meanwhile, the nation was struggling for a redefinition of work, erasing even the faintest reminders of slavery. To distract workers from the oppression of their long working hours, entrepreneurs associated art with labor. "Art labor" was to make work more palatable and more marketable. As Isaac Edwards Clarke said, "In this world all men and women must work; it is the law of life, the only path of progress.

The only choice given is, shall your work be good work, work that you love, work that helps you,and helps the world?"[7] In a commencement address, Clarke, an advocate for art education, actually declared, "The chief message which Art brings the modern life is the announcement of the truth that Labor can be made a delight and a blessing to all."[8]

Redefinition of Art

Art and economic advancement were bonded in the public mind by the last half of the nineteenth century. Signs of it may be read as early as the 1840s when farmers read that drawing "assists the farmer to arrange with taste and beautify his grounds".[9] Periodicals and books argued that work became superior and more valuable if the worker took the time to learn how to draw. Consequently, workers did learn to draw, to plan more carefully, to avoid waste, and to show clients their saleable ideas.

The most prominent art instruction book, published first in 1847 and then reissued through the 1870s, John Gadsby Chapman's *American Drawing-book,* assured its readers, "Drawing has its practical uses in every occupation. It opens inexhaustible sources of utility."[10]

Who Let the Women Go?

Entry into the world of work was the wedge that ultimately created widespread art opportunities for women. Especially in the early days of mill life, work had dignity. With the growth of the industrial cities, families clung together less and the promise of a regular pay check sent women off to worlds about which they and their parents knew nothing. Daughters who never would have found themselves painting and drawing in private girls' seminaries found themselves studying art because it was seen as ultimately contributing to the economy of the family. Reputed to have aesthetic natures and fine hand skills, girls' endowments seemed to make them prime candidates for "art labor" as it came to be known.

For the almost 900 women who attended MNAS in its first 30 years, art school was just one small step further toward an acceptable independence. The way was paved by the Massachusetts legislature that had passed The Drawing Act of 1870. Adults thereby were assured of what was now a right for every school child: "training in art."

Mill cities had the population to justify free evening drawing classes;
Lawrence, Lowell, Springfield, Fall River, Worchester, New Bedford all
had populations over ten thousand. Even after twelve hours of work,
men and women would go to these classes in the evening to learn and
to practice. Not surprisingly, the taste for art developed and students
wanted more. By 1873, their opportunity had come. The MNAS was
explicitly created to allow those avid draughtsmen and women to extend
their skills. It became acceptable for a young woman to go off to
Boston, get a room in a boarding house, and attend daytime drawing
classes at MNAS.

MNAS had high visibility. As early as 1875, the students published a
book, titled *The Antefix Papers*, of presentations originally offered at
weekly meetings of the Massachusetts Art Teachers' Association.
Charles Callahan Perkins, the moving force who saw to the founding of
both MNAS and its partner, Boston's Museum of Fine Arts, was then
Chairman of the Massachusetts Board of Education. Perkins began his
preface to the book:

"The papers here collected were written by many earnest *workers* (my
italics) in a cause which is becoming everyday more important in the
eyes of Americans ...it is the work of men and women *laboring* under
every disadvantage, to fit themselves to be art teachers."[11]

"The cause" according to May Smith Dean, one of Walter Smith's
twelve children, was to remedy the scarcity of information about art,
particularly the lack of art books in America.

The research in the *Antifix Papers* was published without a clue to the
individual authors. Only Smith himself, Perkins, and William R. Ware
are named. Fortunately, in Smith's own copy he penned in the author's
names. Although the first chapter, written by Smith himself, was
entitled, "The Greatness of Great Men," 17 names beginning with
"Miss ..."were authors of the remaining 29 chapters. A sampling of
authors and subjects is listed here. Miss R.L. Hoyt, who recollected
how Smith first brought her to MNAS as a student, wrote "The
Application of Principles of Design to Cast Metal Objects." Miss
N.N. Stuart wrote on "Color —The Origin of Pigments and their
Chemical Action." Miss Mary E. Clapp wrote "Design Applied to
Carved Objects," and Miss A.M. Spalter was the author of "Design

Applied to Printed Fabrics." The papers were not all about technical subjects. Miss Caroline Nolan wrote on "Historic Schools of Painting down to the Seventeenth Century," and Miss E.F. Locke carried the survey forward into the nineteenth century. Miss S. A. Walker wrote "Pottery and Porcelain." The most up-to-date subject was that of Miss L.A. Dudley, who wrote on the technological change that was soon to transform the role of the artist and the diffusion of images in this country, "The Application of Photography to Engraving."

Conclusion

MNAS continued to find accomplished students for its classes. Who were they? More research needs to be done. The history of American art could profitably be expanded by examining the art of women who needed to work. The Boston Museum of Fine Arts exhibition "Bostonians; Artists in an Age of Elegance (1870-1930)" included many women, but few were of the laboring class. None of the 898 female alumnae of the first 30 years of MNAS were included. Of the next 30 years, only one woman, Margaret Fitzhugh Browne, Class of 1908, was represented in the Boston exhibition. Significantly, from the 60 years covered in the exhibition, 12 men with MNAS affiliation, either as students, faculty, or both, were selected.

The exhibition tacitly demonstrated that in Boston, especially for women, there were two rival artistic realities, that of the Boston Museum of Fine Arts School and that of the Massachusetts Normal Art School. Created for two distinctly different social missions, not viewed or even thought about simultaneously, these two visions create a peculiar discomfort if one attempts to merge them. We need to examine both and to pay attention to the difference and the discomfort.

Notes.
1. Walter Smith, *Art Education, Scholastic and Industrial* (Boston: James R. Osgood and Company, 1872), p.28.
2. Ibid.,p.29.
3. Ibid.,p.24.
4. May Smith Dean, *History of the Massachusetts Normal Art School*

1873-4 to 1923-4. Reprinted from ten issue of the MNASAA Bulletin, April 1923 to May 1924, p.7.

5. Ibid., p.22.

6. Ibid., p.28.

7. Isaac Edward Clarke, *Art and Industry, Instruction in Drawing Applied to the Industrial and Fine Arts as given in the Colleges of Agriculture and the Mechanical Arts, and in the Public Schools and other public Educational Institutions in the United States, Vol 1* (Washington, D.C.: Government Printing Office, 1880) p.cxxxv

8. Ibid., p.234

9. Benjamin H. Coe, *Easy Lessons in Landscape Drawing* (Hartford: E.B. and E.C. Kellogg, 1842)

10. John Gadsby Chapman, *The American Drawing-book* (New York; J.Redfield, 1847), p.4.

11. Charles Callahan Perkins, in *The Antefix Papers* (Boston: Printed for Private Circulation, 1875), p.iii.

— **Diana Korzenik**

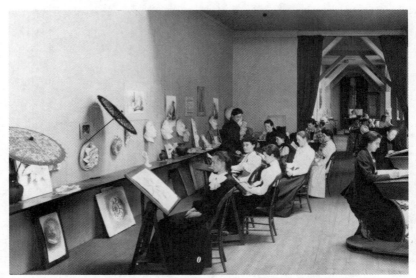

A.H. Folsom photograph of Girls High School Class, 1893, Boston. Courtesy of the Boston Public Library, Print Department.

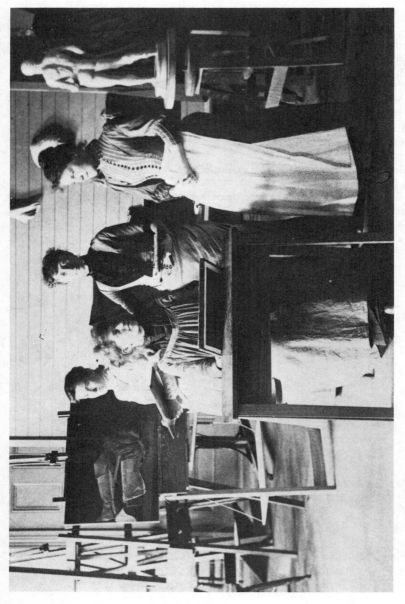

Massachusetts Normal Art School class, 1888. Courtesy Massachusetts College of Art Library Archives.

WOMEN PIONEERS
IN MAINE ART

In December of 1826, a well-dresssed thirty-four year old woman arrived in Portland, where she had been told she could make a living as a portrait painter. Her name was Susanna Paine, and she proceeded to rent a room from Mrs. Margaret Pritchard on Free Street, place a notice in the *Portland Advertiser* and, with her remaining three dollars, wait for customers. When nobody responded, the would-be painter faced financial disaster. Finally, the sensitive Mrs. Pritchard noticed the artist's situation, offered to exchange rent for a portrait and began to promote Miss Paine among her friends. In a short time Paine's work gained recognition, and she was delighted to find a letter printed in the *Advertiser* sympathetic to her and signed, "A Friend of Merit." In part the supporter wrote:

Miss P. is a native of the U.S. . . . a stranger in this place, and was induced to come here on the assurances of finding employment. I know it is too often the case that native genius and talent is too frequently neglected, whilst foreigners are sought after and patronized — such things ought not to be. I think it is only necessary for this person to be known, to be employed. Ladies must feel a pride and pleasure in patronizing a female artist.

Portland was on the threshold of becoming a significant cultural and economic rival of Boston and boasted, or would soon boast, the presence of such painters as Charles Codman, William Matthew Prior, Charles Octavius Cole, Henry Cheever Pratt, and America's pioneer art critic (and vocal advocate of the total equality of women), John Neal (1793-1876). Maine was this critic's place of business, and cultural leaders from Rembrandt Peale to Edgar Allen Poe came to him for assistance, advice, and comment. In the years before 1880, Maine produced such nationally important figures as Henry Wadsworth Longfellow, Sally Wood, Seba Smith, Fanklin Simmons, Alexander Parris, Benjamin Paul Akers, N.P. Willis, and Harrison Bird Brown. The abundance of such talent put the state firmly in the mainstream of American culture. As it turned out, Miss Paine had chosen the right time and place to launch a career.

Susanna Paine was perhaps the original woman pioneer in the field.

During her long career she evolved a strong personal style and traveled the coast and back country, where she became one of New England's best known itinerant painters. In her autobiography, *Roses and Thorns* (1854), she states that her decision to paint was one of financial necessity. Susanna was a divorced woman whose only training came from a female academy. Whereas boys were generally discouraged from careers in art, girls were usually trained in the "ornamental branches of education." While the intent of such art, music, and literature courses was to make them good wives and mothers, it also taught them a practical skill. Women like Susanna Paine, who did not wish to become ornamental themselves, turned such training into a trade. One has only to look at the student watercolors of Ellen and Sarah Moore to see the complex use of media employed, the patiently learned use of drawing, and the curious mixture of stylization and abstraction that emerged from such schools. Women not wishing to marry or teach school were quick to grasp this option. In *Leaflets of Artists* (1893), Annie Eliza Hardy described her aunt Mary Ann Hardy's career:

This work was real work, nerve-trying and wearing, but it was in the line of her tastes and also remunerative, giving her the opportunity of self-support at a time when there was little variety in the occupations of women, and few openings for them to earn money independently.

Few women followed Paine down the itinerant road, although, as Arthur Gerrier of the Maine Historical Society dicovered, Rumford's Caroline Wardwell did so in 1844. In January of that year, Dixfield diarist Persis Andrews recorded:

I have been sitting the past week for my miniature. It is taken with my babe in arms & both are s'd to be good likenesses. The baby's perfect....Miss Wardwell paints as well as any Miniature painter I ever knew tho' she is a beginner & almost entirely self taught. She has boarded with us & asks only $5.00. Her company more than pays for a week's board.

The modern observer must agree with Mrs. Andrews. Wardwell's strong, highly detailed painting ranks her with such skilled miniature painters as Bangor's Mary Ann Hardy and Portland's Xavier Stoppel.

Between the Federal period and World War I, women made up more than half of Maine's painting complement. Many of these artists were amateurs or derived part of their income from painting, but that was true of their male counterparts as well. One cannot conclude that women dominated the cultural scene, but as individuals they played a more important role than is generally believed. One should recall that Sarah Willis Parton's book *Fern Leaves From Fanny's Portfolio* (1853) sold an astonishing 70,000 copies, that Neal ranked Elizabeth Murray among the finest of painters, and that the writer-critic Margaret Jane Mussey Sweat willed her house and the funds to build the Portland Museum of Art, the first public art museum in Maine. Second only to Neal as a critic and promotor of the local art scene was Ann S. Stephens (1813-1886). During the 1830's her *Portland Magazine* combined writing and visual arts criticism "in a small compass."

Women painters existed in abundance. They exhibited with their male contemporaries, were given as much newpaper coverage and critical attention, and played vigorous parts in cultural affairs. Their concerns and approaches seem to have been similar to those of the males. While few of their careers led to wealth, a solid number of women did achieve economic freedom and mobility. Minnie Libby of Norway, who was given a retrospective showing at the Western Maine Art Center in 1981, was "the" town photographer. This trade allowed her to pursue her interest in painting and wildlife. Libby's reputation as an artist rests secure in the community of Norway. Much the same can be said of Bangor's Annie Eliza Hardy, whose flower paintings were widely collected throughout New England and whose work continues to be popular. Current study of Hannah B. Skeele by the Brick Store Museum and Martha Gandy Fales is uncovering the long forgotten talent of one of the area's leading artists of the 1870's. Such projects are likely to bring new understanding of the contemporary reassessment of nineteenth century art, which began in the 1960's.

Also exciting is the location and identification of non-professional artists who may have produced only a few, but very special, images. Roberta Hansen's discovery of Susan Kendall's extraordinary "*Pool Road Paintings*" opened the window on a special world of 1848. Indeed, the pastel views of north Monmouth and Casco by Elizabeth Robinson (c.1862) and Rachel Jordan (c.1855) would not have been considered art by critics including Neal and Stephens. For the present-day student, collector, or scholar, however, they offer an innocent and honest entry into the spirit of the times and stand as major works of folk-art.

While much is known about such prolific painters as Mary Neal Richardson and Nellie B. Walker, the lives and careers of A.B. Wakefield, Ava Park and Eliza McLellan Mayall are virtual blanks. Had Cora Bragdon not signed her magnificent naive oil of Lewiston Falls, there would be no clue that such a person ever existed. Beyond those artists who are known only through a signature on one or two canvases, are once-noted women whose paintings have yet to be accounted for. Local nineteenth century newspaper articles and catalogue notes offer rich documentation of such painters as Miss A.L.P. Skillings, Susan Cloudman, Annie Cloudman Kimball and Lizzie Dyer. But their works seem to have vanished from sight. Even paintings by such prolific and successful professionals as Elizabeth Murray and Maria à Becket rarely escape from attics or storage. It is hoped that further research can restore these "forgotten artists" to their rightful place. When that is done, a fuller, more balanced understanding of Maine's rich, complex, and highly individualistic cultural scene of the last century will take shape.

Contrasting the art and artists of the nineteenth and twentieth centuries in Maine is a rewarding task. Beginning in the 1820s, the nativist landscape school was the dominant concern of painters and local collectors. Portland was the commercial and cultural focus of the region, with Bangor a close second. The American art world itself was a widely decentralized affair composed of flourishing, interconnected, grass roots centers. During this time, women painters made their first deep inroads. Whether their technique was naive or sophisticated, their concerns and subjects were largely indistinguishable from those of the men.[1] Interest in landscape and portraiture predominated and found a ready local market.

Following the Civil War, industrial growth in other parts of the nation overwhelmed Maine's commercial supremacy, and the state began a slow economic and attitudinal decline. Established artists of both sexes clung to their old patrons and continued old styles well into the twentieth century. However, younger artists, with no reasonable expectations of making a living at home, gravitated to Boston and New York. This process was repeated in other declining regions and led to the gradual centralization of the American art scene. By the1880s, self-taught artists, long the dominant type in America, were no longer much in evidence. A formal studio education was now considered almost a necessity. By the same period, prestigious art academies and schools had partially or fully opened to women.[2] Such opportunities were quickly grasped by young Mainers, including South Berwick's Marcia Oakes Woodbury and Presque Isle's Lucy Hayward Barker, who left home for the brave new world of Boston art schools. In the next generation, psychological pressures also worked their spell on young artists like Louise Nevelson, who shed the provincial confines of Rockland for the freedom of New York.

As surely as necessity compelled Down-Easters toward the distant centers of culture, success enabled more established artists to discover Maine. These new arrivals included members of both sexes. Since the time of Thomas Cole, artists had visited Maine on sketching tours of short duration. In1883, however, Winslow Homer had come to Prouts Neck to open a permanent studio far from the pressures of the city. He had a few immediate imitators. There was, of course, no local market in Maine, but the working conditions were splendid for those with big city galleries. By the turn of the century, the nationally successful artist, Maria Oakey Dewing, and her painter-husband Thomas, opened a summer studio near Fryeburg.

The return of Marcia Oakes Woodbury and her husband Charles had wider implications. With reputations already established, they opened a working studio in Ogunquit, and from 1898 to 1917 Charles taught his famous beach-side classes. The Woodburys deserve credit as pioneers of the concept of summer art colonies which sprouted along the coast from Boothbay to Monhegan to Eastport. Unquestionably, this phenomenon both shaped and colored the era under discussion and demands separate, serious treatment.

Artists like the Woodburys helped introduce positive atitudes toward art as well as a style, loosely based on French Impressionism, that was in this county progressive[3] and soon had many adherents. Charles' Ogunquit students included Anne Carleton, Dorothy Emmons, and Nellie Knopf. Working in close harmony with this group were such figures as Gertrude Fiske and Mabel May Woodward, whose impressionistic canvases and forceful personalities added substance to the overall colony. In the winters, such women left the state to teach: Woodward at the Rhode Island School of Design; Knopf at MacMurray College; and Carleton at schools in Marblehead, Needham, and Lynn, Massachusetts. Fiske had her studio in Boston, was a founding member of numerous art societies, and was the first woman appointed to the State Art Commission of Massachusetts. Without question, such active professionals helped expand the role of women artists in local and national culture.

Edith Cleaves Barry, an interesting late progresssive, left an enduring cultural legacy to the state. In 1936, the artist opened Kennebunk's splendid Brick Store Museum and ran a workshop for local artists which endured into the sixties. Other women who were not full-time artists played a sweeping role in establishing collecting institutions. Mary and Harriet Walker funded the first Bowdoin College Museum of Art building (1891); Margaret Jane Mussey Sweat willed her home and money to build what became the Portland Museum of Art (1907); and Lucy Copeland Farnsworth endowed the construction of Rockland's William A. Farnsworth Library and Art Museum (1935). Though all the earliest Maine museums were established by women, the founders chose to name them in honor of male relatives. Thus has polite convention tended to mask the facts. The only Maine museum named for a woman is The Joan Whitney Payson Gallery of Art, founded by John W. Payson and Nancy Lawler Payson in 1977.

Shortly after World War I, a great avant-garde wave swept into Maine. Moderns like Marin, Lachaise, Kuhn, and the Zorachs all responded to the same stark landscape and working conditions that had drawn the progressives. At Ogunquit, Hamilton Easter Field and Henry Strater offered, in turn, a collection and a museum representing the best works of their generation. The new Ogunquit scene was heavily male, with a few talented but overshadowed women like Katherine Schmidt. Avant-garde women appeared in other charmed circles: Sarah McPherson made annual summer trips to Monhegan; Peggy Bacon worked at Ogunquit before making a home at Cape Porpoise; others like O'Keeffe made brief, though artistically significant, forays to the coast. Among the most valuable of the long-term "Mainers by choice" was Marguerite Zorach, who settled with her family at Robinhood in 1923. This Cubist pioneer came to exert a lasting influence on the area. Her daughter, Dahlov Ipcar, grew up in Maine, has made her career in-state, and continues the positive family tradition.

Without question, the men and women who brought modern visions into Maine also enriched attitudes. The weight of their combined talents, however, tended to submerge whole strata of native production. At first, a conservative reaction set in among locals. In Portland, the old center of culture, modern works were attacked by the press in favor of impressionistic landscapes which had only recently been considered suspect. By the late twenties, though, this defensive posture began to shift. Natives, trained in formal settings, had begun to produce more forcefully.

For the first time, numbers of women began to enter the political side of the cultural arena. Among the earliest and most enduring of these was Mildred Burrage. Born in Portland, she studied in Europe and exhibited widely before returning in 1917. From that time through the seventies, she left a heritage of work and social activism that has few equals. A principal force in the Maine Coast Gallery at Wiscasset, she led the fight to save a variety of historic Maine buildings and served later as a director of the National Trust for Historic Preservation.

A fuller understanding of the part played by the Portland School of Art[4] and its influential director, Alexander Bower, is just now emerging. Bower's finest students included Alice Kirkpatrick, Bernice Breck, Roberta DiMatteo and Dorothy Jensen. When Bernice Breck became Secretary of the Portland Society of Art in 1932, she assumed a key role previously granted to men. Her duties included correspondence, bookkeeping, and, during the man-power shortage of World War II, the installation of exhibitions at the Portland Museum of Art. For her part, Dorothy Jensen was the first and only director of the Federal Art Project of the Works Progress Administration of Maine (1935-1942).

This was part of the national government's Depression-era work projects and included men and women in every state. Maine had never seen a project of this scope. As director, Jensen had to select candidates on the basis of merit and need, and then find projects to keep between thirty and forty men and women employed. Murals, posters, illustrations, displays, and even signs were made for public institutions. Some150 paintings of decorative objects located by the director were made for an extraordinary index of American design.[5] The W.P.A. enabled such painters as Flora G. Cullen to continue working in the state. The impact of the program deserves further study.

The coming of World War II saw the end of the W.P.A. and the turning to essential, home-front jobs by women. Burrage, for example, worked as a counselor at the South Portland shipyards where she continued to paint. Important social strides by women took place through 1945, which proved to be one of the true watershed dates in art history. Thereafter, America experienced an attitudinal back-lash toward working women. Though outside the mandate of this study, the next two decades produced few women who were granted critical recognition on a national level.

Thus the paths begun in the nineteenth century were pushed further by new generations. The earlier century had failed to produce any Maine-related artists with stature approaching that of Zorach or Bacon; nor was there anything like the consistent quality that appeared in their time. Documents and works by twentieth-century Maine artists were scattered or embarassingly incomplete until the eighties. Even such generally able surveys as Colby College's *Maine and Its Role in American Art* make only token mention of female artists. That particular work mentions only O'Keeffe, Zorach, Burrage, and Ipcar, and, while no one can dispute that they worked on a higher level than Carelton or Emmons, the work of the latter is no less crucial in gauging the fabric of the time and place. One is left to wonder what became of Bacon, Fiske, or Isabella Howland, let alone the contributions of the W.P.A. It seems evident that cultural historians have not only failed to study women, but have missed a whole level of local endeavor in the process. Such an obvious neglect of our mutually shared heritage has led to an imbalanced view that can be redressed only through a pioneering effort in our time.

Notes:
1. The whole field of decorative arts and utilitarian crafts is a different matter and falls outside the edges of our study.
2. A small number of women, including Maria Oakey Dewing, received training earlier. For a thorough discussion, the reader is directed to Charlotte Streifer Rubinstein's excellent book, *American Women Artists: From Early Indian Times to the Present.* (New York: Avon Books, 1982).
3. The use of the word "progressive" is intended to net a variety of moderate landscape and portrait styles that emerged after the nativist landscape tradition begun by Thomas Cole and prior to the radical intrusion associated with the Armory Show. The styles, which also include a variety of approaches, are termed avant-garde or Modern in this essay.
4. Then called the Portland School of Fine and Applied Art. Together with the L.D.M. Sweat Memorial Museum (now the Portland Museum of Art), they were under the directorship of the Portland Society of Art.
5. The index of American design, a nationwide compilation of portfolios of drawings illustrating early native arts and crafts of the country, was put together by the W.P.A. Examples from that portfolio were later published under the titles of *Index Of American Design* and *Treasury of American Design.*

—William David Barry

This article is adapted from catalogue essays by William David Barry for the exhibitions, Women Pioneers in Maine Art *(December 26, 1981- February 14, 1982) and* Women Pioneers in Maine Art, 1900-1945 *(April 9-May 19, 1985) at the Joan Whitney Payson Gallery of Art, Westbrook College, Portland, Maine. The following list of artists is from the same catalogue.*

NINETEENTH CENTURY WOMEN ARTISTS:
Mehetabel Cummings Proctor Baxter, 1837-1914; Sarah Adams Baxter, 1820-?; Maria à Becket ?-1904; Cora Bragdon (late 19th century); Esteria Butler (Farnham), 1814-1891; Martha Darling, 1806-1883; Harriet Clay Dow Davis, 1839-1924; Chansonetta Stanley Emmons, 1858-1937; Catherine "Kate" Furbish, 1834-1931; Alice J. Hall, 1866-1936; Ann Hall (mid-19th century); Annie

Eliza Hardy, 1839-1934; Mary Ann Hardy, 1809 -1887; Sarah D. Harmon (active 1884-1898); Henrietta Maria Benson Homer, 1808-1884; Fannie Holmes Horne, 1854-1939; Rachel Webb Jordan 1831-1922; Susan Eliza Lowe Kendall, 1828-1895; Minnie Libby, 1863-1947; Mary King Longfellow 1852-1945; Alice A. Manter,1857-1919; Eliza McLellan Mayall, 1822-?; Ellen Plumer Moore, 1825-after 1842; Sarah Jane Moore (Crockett), 1818- after 1842; Jennie Rodbird Morse, 1854-1927; Elizabeth Heaphy Murray, 1815-1882; Susanna Paine, 1792-1862; Eva Allen Parks, 1846-1932; Mary Neal Richardson, 1859-1937; Elizabeth Bradbury Stanton Robinson, 1832-1897; Hannah B. Skeele, 1829-1901; Lydia Ingraham Stone, 1807-1826; Harriet Beecher Stowe, 1811-1896; Catherine Porter Talbot, 1859-1938; Kate Allen Tryon, 1865-1952; A.B. Wakefield (mid-nineteenth century); Nellie B. Walker, 1872-1973; Caroline Hill Wardwell (Barker), 1822-after 1894

TWENTIETH CENTURY WOMEN ARTISTS:
Peggy Bacon, B.1895; Lucy Hayward Barker, 1872-1948; Edith Cleaves Barry, 1884-1969; Bernice Breck, B. 1905; Mildred Giddings Burrage, 1890-1983; Mary B. Call, 1877-1966; Anne Carleton, 1878-1968; Flora G. Cullen, 1896-1982; Maria Oakey Dewing, 1845-1927; Roberta Wright DiMatteo, B. 1915; Dorothy Stanley Emmons, 1891-1960; Gertrude Fiske, 1878-1961; Isabella Howland, 1895-1974; Dahlov Ipcar, B. 1917; Dorothy Hay Jensen, B. 1910; Alice Harmon Shaw Kirkpatrick, B.1913; Nellie Augusta Knopf, 1875-1962; Sarah Freedman McPherson, 1894-1978; Louise Nevelson, B.1900; Georgia O'Keeffe, 1887-1986; Cornelia Sage, 1913-1971; Katherine Schmidt, 1898-1978; Marcia Oakes Woodbury, 1865-1913; Mabel May Woodward, 1877-1945; Marguerite Thompson Zorach, 1887-1968.

Katherine Schmidt, *Broe and McDonald Listen In*, 1937, Collection of the Whitney Museum of American Art, NY.

Marguerite Zorach, *Night Breeze* . Courtesy Kraushaar Galleries, NY

Gertrude Fiske, *Dorcos*, c.1920s. Courtesy Robert Schoelkopf Gallery, NY.

Catherine Beecher and her sister, Harriet Beecher Stowe, co-authored *American Woman's Home*, a very influential home management guide, published 1869.

NEW ENGLAND
WOMEN ARCHITECTS

New England women have contributed significantly to the profession of architecture, beginning in the late nineteenth century and continuing through the twentieth century. Much of this activity centers in the Boston area, since Boston, the largest city in New England, is the hub for educational, cultural, and financial activities.

These women have a rightfully earned reputation for independence, a quality which helped them in pursuing architecture. Though the fine arts were considered suitable activities (if not careers) for women in the nineteenth century, architecture was definitely not since it was a business that involved supervising laborers, visiting construction sites, working in an office, and getting clients. In the early part of the nineteenth century, architectural training was obtained by apprenticing in an architect's office. Toward the end of the century one attended a school of architecture, usually attached to a university, where women were seldom admitted. For all these reasons and others it was difficult for women to enter the field.

Training for architecture was also a problem, since there were very few schools of architecture in New England. The Massachusetts Institute of Technology had to accept women as students as early as the 1880s due to their Land-Grant status, but many women did not feel welcome or comfortable there. In 1915 the Cambridge School of Architecture and Landscape Architecture for women was founded by Henry Atherton Frost and Bremmer Pond. Harvard University also offered architecture, but not to women until 1942, when the Cambridge School closed. The courses at all these schools were long and difficult. A timid woman without a commitment to the profession would be discouraged from applying. However, many women did persevere, not only through their studies, but through their lives, and became leading architects in New England.

The architectural firm of Howe, Manning and Almy began in 1895 and closed in 1937. During the fifty intervening years this Boston firm had approximately 500 projects, primarily residential, including both large and small houses, low-income housing, and housing projects. **Lois Lilley Howe** founded the firm in 1895; **Eleanor Manning** joined the firm in 1913, and **Mary Almy** became the third partner in 1926. All three women received their architectural degrees from the Massachusetts Institute of Technology — Howe in 1890, Manning in 1906, and Almy in 1920. All three had been raised and educated in the Boston area.

Among their achievements were awards, publications, and projects. Howe won second prize in the design competition for the Women's Building at the Columbian Exposition in Chicago in 1893; her experimental exterior plaster work was published in *Architectural Review* and *Architectural Record*. She used her own measured drawings in her book *Details of Old New England Houses*, published in 1913 in collaboration with Constance Fuller, and was elected a Fellow of the American Institute of Architects in 1931. Manning designed the first low-income housing in Boston, Old Harbor Village; taught design at several local colleges; and developed career testing patterns for potential architectural students.

Howe, Manning and Almy were part of the revivalist movement, and their structures unabashedly copied the past. Recreations of early New England clapboard houses and the brick Georgian style were standard in their repertoire. The Frothingham Residence in Cambridge, Massachusetts, was a Georgian style houses they designed in 1922. They occasionally produced a Tudor home, complete with half-timbering, or a stately and simple neo-classical building. There are also a few examples of other styles — a small bungalow, or a hint in their later work of the influence of Art Deco. However, the bulk of the firm's work was completed long before the International Style invaded domestic architecture.

The firm's specialty was domestic architecture — robust, graceful, and typically American houses — but the women also designed commercial spaces, professional clubs, and public housing. They enjoyed "renovising," a term invented by Manning to mean renovating and revising outdated structures. Their style, inspired by classical, Tudor, Georgian, and colonial architecture, has attracted renewed interest and appreciation, as home owners have grown more active in renovating old houses, and as the community has become more concerned about historic architecture and its preservation.

Eleanor Raymond, FAIA, was among the early sudents at the Cambridge School of Architecture and Landscape Architecture for women in Cambridge, Massachusetts. She studied architecture there from 1917 to 1919 and formally received her Master of Architecture degree after Smith College took over the school. Raymond's environmental interests were awakened during her student days at Wellesley College (1905-09), developed at the Cambridge School, and continued throughout her life.

Raymond's energies were devoted primarily to architecture and her architectural practice. Her first buildings were done in partnership with Henry Atherton Frost, who was director of the Cambridge School and professor of architecture at Harvard University. In 1928 she opened her own office in Boston and practiced until her retirement in 1973 at the age of eighty-five. Her last project was completed that year in Maine for her longtime client, Mary Byers Smith.

Raymond was a pioneer in contemporary architectural design, energy conservation, environmental compatibility, technical innovation, and coloration. The 1931 Raymond House in Belmont, Massachusetts, was featured in *Architectural Forum* magazine as the first house in New England to be built in the International Style. In 1948 Raymond and Dr. Maria Telkes of the Massachusetts Institute of Technology received national recognition for their Dover Sun House, heated exclusively by solar energy. Raymond also experimented successfully with new materials in her Plywood House and Masonite House of the 1940s. For her design abilities, Raymond was elected a Fellow of the American Institute of Architects in 1961.

Her projects, although primarily residential, included an artist's studio, a factory, a piggery, and stables. Raymond believed in the importance of practicing domestic architecture — of providing people with healthful and livable dwellings. Within the context of domestic architecture she investigated and solved major architectural issues of aesthetics, technology, and function. Her work is essential to understanding the past and the future of New England architecture.

Sarah Pillsbury Harkness, FAIA, was among the last graduates from the Cambridge School of Architecture and Landscape Architecture, receiving her Master of Architecture in 1940, one and a half years before the school was closed and women were admitted to Harvard. Like many of her colleagues, her professional opportunities and career expanded to meet her inherent skills and ambitions. Economic and social changes brought on by World War II and continuing through the next forty years increased opportunities for women to enter professions and businesses. Sarah Harkness, along with other women, was integrated into the male work world with opportunities to have both male and female colleagues, coworkers, and clients. The civil rights legislation of the 1960s forced businesses (and governmental agencies) to hire women architects. The life of Sarah Harkness reflects these social and economic changes, which transformed the lives of many women in the United States. She married an architect, with whom she worked for over 40 years, and had seven children, in addition to her career. Such a life pattern was unthinkable for earlier women architects.

In 1945 Harkness and her husband, along with five other young architects, joined Walter Gropius to form The Architects Collaborative. Another of the architects was also a woman: **Jean Fletcher.** Walter Gropius was head of the Harvard Department of Architecture and was internationally known as the founder of the Bauhaus in Germany. The firm has grown from the original eight members to over two hundred, designing major projects in New England, throughout the United States, and many foreign countries. TAC is part of corporate America, and Sarah Harkness has been active shaping that corporate structure.

Harkness' first architectural commission was in 1942, a summer house for her parents in Duxbury, Massachusetts. Harkness worked in Raymond's office, and this house was accomplished under the watchful eye of Eleanor Raymond. Recent Harkness projects have included the North Shore Community College in Beverly, Massachusetts, the Art School at the Worchester Art Museum, and four buildings at Bates College in Lewiston, Maine. The Olin Arts Center is one of the buildings completed at Bates College in 1985. Harkness' architectural activities have encompassed research and publications on solar design, barrier-free buildings for the disabled, energy conservation, and her recent publication, *Sustainable Design for Two Maine Islands.* The respect and admiration of Harkness' clients and colleagues have been demonstrated by the honorary degree awarded her by Bates College in

1974 and by her election as president of the Boston Society of Architecture in 1985.

In 1973 my book *From Tipi to Skyscraper, A History of Women in Architecture* (Boston: i press) addressed the question, "Why should a woman be an architect?" With aditional articles and books, actions, exhibitions, and architectural projects by women that question should now be answered. The woman architect's professional place has become more accepted, providing new career opportunities and expanded responsibilities. My own career reflects the diverse opportunities of architecture, with seven years as staff architect for project programming at the Massachusetts Institute of Technology before opening my own office, Cole and Goyette, Architects and Planners Inc., with Harold Goyette, AIA, AICP, in 1979. My diversified practice encompasses public housing, technical soundproofing, educational buildings, and the redesign of the corporate headquarters for L.S. Thorpe Company, Inc. in Somerville, Massachusetts, in 1986.

The 1985 Boston Society of Architects Exhibition of Women Architects included work by 51 women ranging from private residences to schools, multifamily housing, and nearly every building type. Women's participation in designing the built environment has greatly expanded and developed since the turn of the century. Many New England women architects have formed new partnerships and corporations or become principals and associates of established firms. Among them are **Melissa Bennett**, chair and founder of the Boston Society of Architects Women in Architecture Committee, who has become an associate with A. Anthony Tappe and Associates Inc.; and **Elizabeth Padjen**, AIA, who has joined her father as a principal at Padjen Associates. Women are still less than 5 percent of registered architects in the United States; for example, as of 1984 there were 3,500 registered architects in Massachusetts, of whom only 150 were women. However, New England women architects are remarkably active, vocal, and influential for their numbers.

—**Doris Cole**

WOMEN AND GALLERIES IN ——— BOSTON: PAST AND PRESENT ———

In their long and complicated involvement with the visual arts in
Boston, women have been numerous in the gallery business. After
World War I, there was a great sense of new possibilities, including a
liberation of women's energies which appeared in every facet of the art
world. Women were artists, gallery owners, framers, and dealers in art
supplies. They sponsored city-wide events, like the Boston Arts
Festival, the New Years Eve celebration and First Night, and women
were also active in historic associations like the Copley Society
(founded 1879) and the Society of Arts and Crafts (1897).

Their impetus was involvement with the cultural life of the
community. They started galleries with idealistic intentions: to work
with the arts, to help artists, to educate the public. Of course some of
the women proved to be good business people and pursued sales
aggressively— to the gratitude of their artists.

The Beginnings

In the late 19th century there were some half-dozen art and frame shops
in Boston, the predecessors of today's galleries. When the Grace Horne
Gallery appeared in the early twenties, it was similar enough to two
established galleries to be well received. (Boston continued to prefer
nineteenth century traditions well into the twentieth century.)
Although it started conventionally, the Horne Gallery seems to have
taken the first small steps into modernism that led to the much bolder
ones of Margaret Brown 20 years later.

Grace Horne had grown up in Cambridge. She studied music and
became Supervisor of Music in the Watertown schools. But during
vacations she studied art in East Gloucester, where she opened a little
shop around 1920. By 1922, she had a gallery on Stuart Street in
Boston, which grew rapidly and prospered, employing several people.
It showed contemporary work from New England and elsewhere, taking
the art on consignment and charging a one-third commission on sales.
The gallery's regular artists included several women— Molly Luce,
Helen Dickson, Esther Williams, and others. It also represented many
prominent male artists of the time and was said to have discovered the
landscape artist, John Whorf. There was a strong tradition of watercolor

in Boston, stemming from Winslow Homer, and several watercolorists were supported by the gallery. Grace Horne died in 1934, but the gallery continued for almost another decade under her manager. Horne's obituary (Feb. 17, 1934) noted that the gallery was internationally known and had introduced many young artists to the public.

In 1935, still flourishing, Grace Horne Gallery moved to Newbury Street, where the narrow old houses with shops at street level were an established center of art activity. Three large rooms made it the largest gallery in Boston, and soon a print room was added. Now sales were made to architects and corporations as well as to private collectors and museums, including the Museum of Fine Arts. Maud Morgan, then a New Yorker, exhibited there in 1938. In 1941 the gallery moved to the upper floor of the declining Boston Art Club. With the approach of World War II, however, it came upon hard times, fell into debt, lost its manager, and finally closed in 1943.

The Forties

Generally speaking, the Boston art world was small during the forties, but in January 1945 an association of galleries produced a number of concurrent exhibitions as "The Panorama of Modern Art." These were the Mirski, Charles E. Smith, Today's Art Gallery, and the Stuart Art Gallery.

The Stuart Gallery was owned by a woman, Jean B. Deering, who was assisted by Esther Geller, a young artist. Deering is said to have been a striking figure, soft-spoken, but tall and flamboyant in appearance. Her gallery, lasting at least from 1944 to 1949, gave an imposing first show to Hyman Bloom, and exhibited Provincetown painters and northeastern artists including Charles Hopkinson, Carl Pickhardt, and Dorothy Segal. It also presented international art. A colorful Surrealist exhibition with work by Salvador Dali, Yves Tanguey and others was considered so extreme by the Boston Globe that it was featured on the front page, with photos of Jean Deering and Esther Geller (much to the horror of Geller's parents).

The Margaret Brown Gallery

By 1944 Margaret Brown had founded her own gallery, first as an art and frame shop, later as a gallery in Dartmouth Street. Educated at

Brighton Academy and the Brooklyn Art School, Brown was by all accounts a beautiful and vibrant young woman — forceful, enthusiastic, and persuasive about contemporary art. She soon had a devoted following. The avant garde artists she exhibited included Franz Kline, Willem de Kooning, Alexander Calder and David Smith, as well as Karl Zerbe, Gregory and Juliet Kepes, Steven Trefonides, Lawrence Kupferman, Ruth Cobb, Katherine Sturgis Goodman and Robert Neuman. With close ties to Betty Parsons and Marian Willard in New York, Brown was able to present the best work while it was new. Other Boston galleries preferred the contemporary Boston Expressionist school, as exemplified by Bloom, Levine and Aronson, so her gallery was a mecca for abstract work. Sales were brisk, especially, one suspects, for the less radical works, to a clientele that included old and new money, WASP and Jew. Brown also succeeded in placing Boston art in Whitney Museum annuals, Carnegie Internationals, and other important group shows, and in selling work to major museums.

All this came to an end in 1957 with Margaret Brown's untimely death at the age of 49. Many who remember her gallery fondly believe it has never been replaced. A memorial exhibition at the DeCordova Museum of works she had shown and sold over the years included, in addition to the artists mentioned, Morris Graves, Alberto Giacometti, Gaston Lachaise, Maud Morgan, Mark Tobey, and Jack Wolfe. Charles Childs wrote the catalogue introduction, saying in part:

She supplied confidence to some who lacked it — impetus and clear vision to those who wanted assurance and direction, and, above all, strength and steadiness to any who were faint-hearted or impatient. Those years Margaret came close to her artists and they gave in return a loyalty that few art dealers could ever earn or own.

The Sixties

American art was now triumphant worldwide, as was reflected in galleries everywhere. A number of New England women founded galleries at that time that are no longer with us: Joan Peterson, Dorothea Weeden, Eleanor Rigelhaupt, and Obelisk, a partnership of Phyllis Rosen and Joan Sonnabend. However, the galleries of Portia Harcus and Barbara Krakow, also dating from that time, are still very much with us.

Joan Peterson came to Boston in 1956. She studied art history at Brown University and painting at the Rhode Island School of Design, worked at the Nexus Gallery, then in 1960 opened a gallery under her own name on Newbury Street. She showed regional artists and nationally known artists like Brooks, Marca-Relli, and Calder. She liked Abstract Expressionism and exhibited two Boston artists who are still active: Jack Wolfe and Jo Sandman. In 1961, Joan Peterson's gallery cooperated with M.I.T. on a Computer Graphic Show. It continued in business until the late seventies.

The Eleanor Rigelhaupt Gallery was another attraction on Newbury Street in the sixties. It lasted about 10 years, carrying contemporary paintings and work reflecting an interest in art and technology. Albert Alcalay, Catherine Zimmerman, and John Townsend were among those represented.

The Mary Harriman Gallery was on Newbury Street for about five years, where it showed Will Barnet and Elise Asher, among others. Origins Gallery, directed by Edith Schulman, showed primitive art, also on Newbury Street.

Dorothea Weeden, a writer living in New Hampshire, started a small gallery in Concord, New Hampshire, in the mid-sixties. When a Newbury Street space became available, she moved to Boston, where she continued to show New Hampshire and regional artists, and gained a reputation for distinctive taste and integrity. Betsy Van Buren, who had studied painting and worked at M.I.T. with sculptor Al Duca, joined her as partner the first year in Boston. Within a few years the gallery moved to a large space on the newly developed Lewis Wharf. It did well there, carrying both private and corporate clientele to this comparatively exotic location. By 1972, however, the space had become too expensive. That year Weeden and Van Buren organized a large traveling show from Ireland that toured U.S. museums, but Weeden's health was failing and the show was her last major effort . In 1978 Van Buren opened her own gallery in Cambridge for a new group of artists.

Nova, an artists' cooperative gallery, formed around 1955 on Stanhope Street and lasted until about 1960. Two young women who had worked there, Phyllis Rosen and Joan Sonnabend, opened their own gallery,

Obelisk, after Nova's demise. Rosen had studied art history in Heidelberg and Sonnabend had attended Sarah Lawrence College. Their attractive small gallery on Newbury Street showed regional and national contemporary artists, including Deborah Remington, Ed Giobbi, Richard Merkin, and Lionel Kipp. They also became acquainted with younger artists then beginning to come to Boston, such as Elizabeth Dworkin and Anthony Thompson. These artists were not tied to Boston traditions as artists of earlier galleries had been.

Meanwhile, another women's gallery, Harcus-Krakow, had become prominent on Newbury Street. It showed the elegant prints created by famous Americans that brought a revival of ateliers and spurred an expanding market of collectors. Barbara Krakow and her husband had been print collectors, buying especially the 20th century master prints that were then easily available in Europe. Portia Harcus had become interested in prints on a trip to Europe.

The Parker Street Experiment and the Seventies

With increasing demand to show emerging Boston artists whose work was too large for narrow Newbury Street spaces, Harcus-Krakow and Obelisk joined forces in 1970 to start a large gallery in a neighborhood of lower rents. While the original Newbury street gallery continued to operate with the types of work previously shown, Parker 470 was founded near the Museum of Fine Arts in a handsome two-story space, a sort of mini-Guggenheim Museum, ample enough for the large canvases of the time. This proved the perfect environment for the developing talent of Katherine Porter, who was Boston's most important artist in years and a strong influence on other artists. The gallery also exhibited Andrew Tavarelli, Robert Rohm, Wolf Kahn, Philip Pearlstein, and Natalie Alper, among others.

Artists probably appreciated Parker 470 more than the Boston art public did. The gallery inspired ventures into warehouse-type spaces in other cities. Discussion meetings encouraged by the dealers grew into regular events attracting large numbers of artists, which led to the establishment of the Boston Visual Artists Union. The director of the Boston Museum of Fine Arts, Perry Rathbone, was invited to speak and listen to artists' complaints about their exclusion from that institution. These were sufficiently persuasive to elicit the promise of the appointment of the first curator of contemporary art for the museum.

Unfortunately, the neighborhood was too hostile an environment. After a series of break-ins and harassments the gallery closed in 1974, returning to Newbury Street and a grander space as Harcus Krakow Rosen Sonnabend. Near the public garden and the Ritz Hotel, it now has several rooms on the main and lower floors, allowing two simultaneous exhibitions, usually one regional, the other by an artist of national reputation. As the leading gallery of the city, it has shaped tastes and developed careers, showing the color field work favored by the curator of contemporary art at the Museum of Fine Arts, Kenworth Moffett— for example: Jules Olitski, Friedel Dzubas, and the young Boston Painter, Sandi Slone. There was also sculpture by Beverly Pepper and Anthony Caro and painting by Neil Welliver, Alex Katz and Pat Steir. Representational Boston artists Susan Shatter, Joel Janowitz, and Michael Mazur developed their careers here, too. Another strong woman, Barbara Divver, was with the gallery for a time, then left to become a private dealer in New York. Sonnabend left to become a private dealer in Boston, Rosen to become an appraiser and consultant. The gallery lasted as Harcus Krakow until 1983, when Barbara Krakow left to open a gallery of her own.

Sunne Savage studied art and art history in the Midwest and came to Boston in the late sixties. She began as an art dealer on Beacon Street in 1970, then opened a gallery on Newbury Street. She exhibited a large range of Boston and New England artists who had no previous gallery exposure. To expand the art public she started "Art Newbury Street," a Sunday afternoon each Spring and Fall when the street was given over to pedestrians and most of the galleries were open. This became an institution and is now one of the few activities in which Newbury Street dealers cooperate. In 1983 Sunne Savage became a private dealer, increasingly interested in nineteenth and early twentieth century art.

The Impressions Gallery on Dartmouth Street, a descendent of the well-known Impressions Print Workshop on Stanhope Street, opened in 1978 and began showing a wider range of works on paper. In 1980 Victoria Munroe added a curator of ceramics, Maria Friedrich, at the moment when there was a surge of interest in that medium. While still running the Boston Gallery, Monroe dealt privately in prints in New York. Seeing the greater opportunities there, she closed the Impressions Gallery in 1983 and opened Victoria Munroe Gallery in New York. Friedrich also moved to New York, as a private dealer in ceramics.

Art Asia, specializing in the arts of Japan, was started by Linda Abegglen and Nitza Rosofsky in Cambridge in 1967; Abegglen moved the gallery to Newbury Street in Boston, where it survived until 1980. Its mission was to display and explicate the subleties of Japanese ceramics, woodcuts and folk arts.

Betsy Magnuson Lee opened another print gallery on Newbury Street in 1980. Despite prestigious exhibitions by "name" artists, the gallery survived only a few years, after which Lee also became a private dealer.

The Congress Street Experiment

In the late seventies two young women who had attended the Museum of Fine Arts School, Bess Cutler and Pat Stavaridis, started a corporate art business, mainly promoting their former teachers' work. They wanted a space larger than their small office, preferably one where artist Cutler could also have a studio. Helen Shlien, who had worked with the Boston Visual Artists Union, was also looking for a gallery space that could accomodate performances and installations. In 1978 the women took the fifth floor of a former factory on Congress Street, in the Fort Point Channel neighborhood toward South Boston. Several artists had studios in the area, and the Atlantic Gallery, run by artists Jane and Jeff Hudson, had existed there briefly.

The Congress Street galleries, with large spaces and 12-foot ceilings, allowed the most grandiose work, and the low rentals of the first years made risk-taking possible. Both Cutler-Stavaridis and Helen Shlien introduced numerous young artists, including John McNamara and Roger Kizik, who were making enormous abstract paintings. The performance and installation room of the Helen Shlien Gallery presented mixed media spectacles and the remarkable installation of Michael Timpson , Nancy Selvage, Penelope Jencks, Steve Wood, and others. A private gallery and an artists' co-op opened in the building.

Opening receptions were gala events that attracted crowds of artists, students, and a handful of collectors. But the general art public would not go so far off course, so attendance between openings was sparse. By 1983, the owners began to feel that their artists needed Newbury Street exposure. Bess Cutler left for New York, where she opened a Soho gallery, while Stavaridis and Shlien moved to Newbury Street. Stavaridis continues; the Shlien Gallery lasted only two more years.

The Eighties

There are many other galleries and art enterprises run by women in Boston today. The Copley Society, which has been on Newbury Street longer than anyone can remember, is directed by Terese Tapani. The gallery of the Society for Arts and Crafts, directed by Herta Loeser, has been on Newbury Street since 1933. Other crafts galleries on Newbury Street include Alianza, opened by Karen Rotenberg and her husband, which originally focused on Mexican and Latin American furniture and artifacts, but has since become a showcase for U.S. craftspeople. Rotenberg also worked devotedly for the Institute of Contemporary Art during more than 20 years as committee member and trustee. Westminster Gallery, directed by Julie Mansfield emphasizes European crafts, while Bunnell, run by Deborah Brown, and Wenniger Graphics, run by Mary Ann Wenniger, are traditional framing and print galleries. In 1983 Francesca Anderson, an art historian who worked for the Shore Gallery, opened a gallery on Newbury Street specializing in New England representational painters. High quality American crafts are shown in Cambridge at 10 Arrow Street Shop and Gallery, opened in 1972 by Elizabeth Tinlot.

Two galleries show the work of black artists. 17 Wendell Street, started in the seventies, is a semi-private gallery run by Jane Shapiro and Constance Brown from Shapiro's house in Cambridge. It specializes in local and early twentieth century artists. The proprietors started as collectors, as did Liz Harris, director of Harris Brown Gallery, opened on Columbus Avenue in 1984. It specializes in nationally known black artists from outside New England, and African art.

An anomalous establishment on Newbury Street for many years was the Edna Hibel Gallery, named for the painter of big-eyed children, young women in white dresses and such. Her mother started the gallery to show Hibel's work, which was soon produced in editions and reproductions. The artist now lives in Florida, where a museum is said to have been established in 1976 to show her work, and now exhibits a group of artists. The Judy Rotenberg Gallery on Newbury Street was also established to show the owner's work, but Rotenberg follows a family tradition, since her mother ran a studio shop on Bolyston Street to sell her father's paintings.

Women have also been active as private dealers. In the late sixties and early seventies, Mildred Lee, a former collector, was the only authorized dealer in the area for Universal Limited Art Editions. There are also Madeline Carter, Sunne Savage, and Joan Genser, a transplanted Candian who uses her house for a showcase and does a large-volume print business. In addition many women are art consultants; Cregier-Sesen, Ginsberg-Hallowell, and Aptekar Associates, to mention only a few. On Charles Street there is Gallery 52, a street-level space, directed by Alison Richter, who started with a partner, Stephanie Hobart, but has been sole owner since 1985. She shows emerging artists of the Boston area.

Going outside of Boston, always problematic for a serious gallery in the region, there is Van Buren/Brazelton/Cutting Gallery in Cambridge, opened in1978. With a generous space and wide interests the gallery has intoduced such new talent as Edie Read and Maxine Yalovitz-Blankenship, as well as showing established artists such as sculptor William Wainwright.

Farthest afield geographically is Clark Gallery in Lincoln, opened in 1976 by three women; Eleanor Clark, a social worker from an art-collecting family, Grace Nichols, also a social worker, and Merydith Hyatt Moses, the energetic director who has performed the almost impossible feat of promoting and selling contemporary art in the suburbs. There is a regular stable of 18 artists, augmented by exchanges with galleries in other cities and in group shows. Younger artists are often featured, but the gallery also carries a range of less difficult work, especially in ceramics.

The eighties have been a turbulent time for the visual arts, with perhaps a new art movement each season. In New York, whole neighborhoods of galleries have opened and many that seemed established have closed. In Boston there have been fewer revolutions. But in the eighties European art has regained its prestige, so we are colonized by branches of foreign galleries.

One of these is Artconsult International, Inc., owned by Carmen Aleman de Carrizo. A graduate of Smith College, she started an international art consulting firm in Panama, then opened a gallery there. Finding herself in Boston, where her husband is Panamanian consul, she opened a branch of the gallery that moved to Newbury Street in 1986. She shows Latin American artists plus a few U.S. artists of Latin descent.

Tina Petra, formerly curator of the Graham Gund collection, is the Boston partner of the Hartje Gallery on Monsignor O'Brien Highway, a branch of the gallery of the same name in Frankfort, West Germany. Founder Katrina Hartje is an American who lives in Germany. The gallery, showing mostly Frankfort artists and a few from Boston, will concentrate on international art fairs.

Portia Harcus' Harcus Gallery is now on South Street, in what used to be the Leather District, a neighborhood discovered by artists some time ago. The gallery's renovated quarters occupy a series of rooms, separated elegantly by massive marbelized columns. As in the past, it has the look of a major gallery— sleek, prosperous, and staffed by well-informed assistants. It continues to show New York and Boston work, following current trends at a slight remove. Well-known artists include Alex Katz, Neil Welliver, and Pat Steir, and Boston artists George Nick, Valta Us, Marcia Lloyd, and Joel Beck. Harcus also directs a small gallery for landscape and other representational work in Charles Square, Cambridge.

Barbara Krakow, her former partner, now has her own fifth-floor gallery on Newbury Street. The handsome space exhibits a few Boston artists and numerous mid-career New York artists, plus an occasional international show, or an older artist with connections to the present day. Susan Rothenberg, Jim Dine, Michael Mazur, Flora Natapoff, and

Catherine Bertulli show there. The gallery has the custom of unpacking work for future shows and displaying it informally among whatever the current show may be, thus creating flux and activity instead of the customary pristine atmosphere. Much of the art is of high quality and reflects the diversity and activity of the larger art scene.

Going from the Barbara Krakow to the Stavardis Gallery is to leave the scene of high-powered dealing for the simpler one of art that has appealed personally to a director. Almost all the work Pat Stavaridis shows is created in the Boston area and is its first exhibition. As Cutler-Stavaridis, the Gallery showed work that could perhaps be described as art with an awareness of what other advanced artists were doing. Stavaridis has to a degree continued that image. Several of her young artists, notably Adam Cvijanovic and Alfonse Borysewicz, do extremely ambitious work and have received unusual recognition from local institutions. Others represented include Al Rizzi, Pat Cooney, and Jack Clift.

The Nielsen Gallery on Newbury Street, opened in 1964, has become an established local institution. Director Nina Nielsen comes from a family of collectors and studied art history at the University of Vienna. The gallery started as a print and frame shop, then became a print gallery specializing in German Expressionists and twentieth century masters. Nielsen began to exhibit paintings and sculpture in 1973, starting with a few artists and increasing to about 20. She is stongly committed to her artists, chosen to conform to her aesthetic rather than to cover the spectrum of art produced at any given time. These include Paul Rotterdam, Joan Snyder, Gregory Amenoff, and Jon Imber, among others.

Women run more than half the galleries in the Boston area; indeed, the local art scene would be barren without them. Despite constant financial pressure, the joys of discovering new work, the sharing with others, and the contact with artists are deeply rewarding and, fortunately, the joys have outweighed the difficulties for many women. By bringing new art to light and explicating it they have furthered its development. Many would agree with Nina Nielsen, who said, "My gallery is my life."

— **Helen Shlien**

PART TWO

CONTEMPORARY
NEW ENGLAND
WOMEN ARTISTS

Molly Upton, *Watchtower*, 1975.

THE QUILT AS ART FORM
IN NEW ENGLAND

New England women have always made quilts. The designing and making of quilts, an indigenous American art form, was much more than just colorful functional artisanry; it was and still is a serious means of artistic expression. Quilts are women's artistic totems. In the past, quilts reflected the hardy female spirit that helped build a country from raw wilderness. Quilts were appealing, sensual, resilient, in a time that left little if any room for a female sensibility. Quilts were a way for women, individually and collectively, to touch concerns of the heart and spirit. In many communities, quilts were the only art, whether identified as such or not, that people ever saw. The most talented quiltmakers from 1800 to 1900 were more than just fabric artists; they were accomplished draftspersons, colorists, and textile architects. Many of the earliest and best quilts were made by women who could not read or write, yet their quilts involved the most sophisticated mathematical understanding. These women knew very well what they were about; they were in no way anonymous.

Quiltmaking flourished even in periods when quilts were not accepted as either decorative or historically significant art. While original and stunning quilts were made in New England from 1900 to 1950, the majority made after the twenties were replicas of work by our foremothers a century before, with little exploration of new design or technique. In the fifties one was more likely to find old quilts used to wrap furniture in moving vans (a common practice) than treated as treasured artifacts.

This changed with the coming of the second wave of the women's movement in the late sixties and early seventies. Young women especially began to seek the roots of women's art and to understand that quilts played a major role in women's art history. Women artists making quilts at this time demanded that quilts be accepted as the legitimate art form they are.

In 1975, **Radka Donnell**, a Bulgarian-born painter who had lived and worked in the United States for many years and given up painting to make quilts full time, was asked by the Carpenter Center for the Visual

Arts at Harvard University to mount an exhibit of her contemporary quilts. Donnell invited two brisk and energetic young women artists, **Molly Upton** (1953-1977) and **Susan Hoffman,** whose brilliant quilts had impressed her, to show with her. The exhibit, "Patchworks," attracted a great deal of attention.

But Donnell did more than design and make modern quilts. She worked tirelessly as an artist and feminist to see quilts taken seriously as an art form — which was no easy task. About her decision to abandon painting and design quilts full time she said:

"In the quilts I had found good objects — hospitable, warm, with soft edges, yet resistant, with boundaries yet suggesting a continuous safe expanse, a field that could be bundled, a bundle that could be unfolded, a portable environment, light, washable, long-lasting, colorful, versatile, functional and ornamental, private and universal, mine and thine. Making the quilts was technically easy, physically rewarding and socially liberating."[1]

Donnell's quilts were bold and abstract, with challenging visual matrices and a powerful weightlessness. Early on, she made the decision to have the pieces machine-quilted on an industrial quilting machine, a decisive and deliberate step away from the traditional hand-quilted surface so much associated with conventional pieced quilts. Responding to the intense criticism this evoked she said:

"The resistance to my quilts came, among other things, from the fact that for this art form, as in other fields held down by the name of crafts, value is associated with excessive demands on the time of women....For my part, I find that the question, 'How long did it take you to make one?' — a question apparently intended to measure a value and dedication otherwise uncomprehended — is plainly sadistic, a sign of disregard for the lifetime of women generally. . . If I had to quilt them by hand I would never have developed a whole body of work expressing the different issues which occupied me, nor would I have reached so many people with my work."

Molly Upton and Susan Hoffman were equally adamant about wanting to show their work on an equal basis with so-called Fine Art. Like Radka Donnell, they had broken out of the constraints of conventional quiltmaking; they used unheard-of combinations of fabrics and techniques and created an architectural style of constructing some quilts that was utterly unique. Between 1974 and 1977, they resolutely knocked on gallery doors and demanded to be recognized . Hoffman was eventually represented by the Kornblee Gallery in New York, and before Upton's tragic death in 1977, the two women had a successful show at the prestigious Smith Anderson Gallery in San Francisco.

There is hardly a contemporary quiltmaker in the United States who has not been influenced one way or another by Radka Donnell, Molly Upton, and Susan Hoffman.

Their exhibit at the Carpenter Center in 1975 was followed by an exhibit of contemporary quilts at the DeCordova Museum the next spring. Then in 1976, in conjunction with the Bicentennial celebration, an open quilt exhibit was hung in the huge cyclorama of the Boston Center for the Arts. Other talented modern quiltmakers surfaced. A supportive community of contemporary quiltmakers began to form that still exists. Today, considerable support for professional quiltmaker/artists comes from the New England Quilters Guild, which had some 2000 members in 1986.

In fact, since 1976, New England has claimed more notable quiltmakers than any other region in the country. Using piecing, appliqué, combination construction, and strip-piecing; using hand and machine quilting as well as graphic and photographic techniques, sometimes combined with hand-painting and direct dye application, the following artists have created an impressive body of work: In Massachusetts, Radka Donnell, **Nancy Halpern, Ruth McDowell, Rhoda Cohen, Barbara Crane, Nell Cogswell, Mary Lou Smith, Nancy Crasco, Susan Turbak, Sylvia Einstein, Alexandra Zallen, Janet Elwin, Judith Larzelere, Linda Levin, Sharon Jeffery,** and **Susan Thompson** are active and important. In New Hampshire, **Tafi Brown** has made a name for herself with photographic quilts depicting architectural subjects. In Vermont, **Jan Norris, Leslie Fuller,** and **Ruth Smiler** have all received a number of distinctions. In Connecticut, **Vikki Chennette**'s work is well known. In Maine, **Elizabeth Busch**, **Gayle Frass**, and **Duncan Slade** are doing notable work.

One wonders then, why it is so difficult to find appropriate formal spaces in which to exhibit large shows of contemporary quilts and why only one quiltmaker, a man, has received a substantial Arts Council Grant.

Clearly, despite the vast number of contemporary art quilts being designed and made, quiltmakers still fail to garner their fair share of recognition from the established art community.

Long shut out, formally and informally (one local painter continues to inquire how my "little" quilts are coming), from the organized art establishment (primarily painters and sculptors), quiltmakers and other textile artists have responded in several ways. For a while in the mid- and late seventies, when I was putting together *The Contemporary Quilt: New American Quilts and Fabric Art* (E.P. Dutton, 1978), the first visual book to deal with other than antique quilts, I noticed to my sorrow that some of the best quiltmakers in the country were describing their work in rambling art babble terms like "machine-constructed, texturally manipulated wall works," "tapestries," "pieced, constructed, embellished, stitched assemblages," and "fabric paintings." They were careful to avoid the word "quilt" or "quiltmaker," since they had learned painfully that to identify their work as what it was meant automatic dismissal as not being "real" art.

Fortunately, this apologizing for quilts did not last long. Quiltmakers began to deal directly with the art/crafts dichotomy by pushing harder and harder against the condescension they had endured. They continued to stay with the historical as well as the artistic integrity of the work, and they continued to make quilts and not concessions. Radka Donnell says of this period:

"The artists and critics among my male acquaintances and friends visibly liked my quilts, but had trouble with them intellectually. Only women painters traded pieces with me, though only a few of them without the sense of an unequal deal. They are right, for, with all due respect to women painters anywhere, quilts are in a class by themselves among objects."

Still, there is more to the problem than an art/craft controversy. Something all too familiar goes much deeper and affects all women. More than anything, it is sexism, not just elitism, that has kept quilts from a share of space on museum walls. Quilts, after all, have been and still are made almost exclusively by women in a culture where the work, concerns, and accomplishments of women are inexorably dismissed as meaningless and unimportant.

Nevertheless, the best New England quiltmakers have continued to move forward, proudly identifying themselves as quiltmakers, assuming it is understood that this means that they are artists who make quilts, and who deserve the full and unqualified support of the art community. With or without that support, quilts as an art form are here to stay.

Note
1. All quotes from Radka Donnell are from an unpublished, untitled manuscript. Reprinted by permission.

— **Pattie Chase**

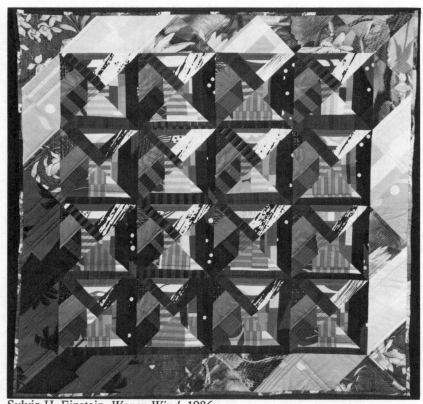

Sylvia H. Einstein, *Woven Wind*, 1986.

Radka Donnell, *A Rose is a Rose is a Rose*, 1986.

Mags Harries, *Glove Cycle* (detail), 1985.

SCULPTURE:
THE SITE AND SPACE

Asked to contribute some thoughts on contemporary sculpture, I found
the choice of focus on environmental work easy. It is my own work,
and issues peculiar to it have been major investigations for me as
curator and teacher. I begin with a question of space: the space of a
sculpture itself; the optical or pyschological presence beyond physical
boundaries; the site space; and the space of the people affected by it.
The diverse artists whose work I discuss bring forward realizations of
space which are increasingly critical as opportunities for environmental
or public art expand.

An important aspect of women's sculpture is innovation. As I talked
with the sculptors, I was reminded of the break-throughs, the "firsts,"
accomplished by some of them. Their achievements are eclectic: in
media, technology, and perception. The range of sculptural content and
materials of these artists, however, precludes their existence as a group.
There are some common convictions and investigations, but these are
more triangular sharings than circular beliefs. What we do share, of
course, is the legacy of sculptural history. Three important items of
this inheritance are the elimination of the sculpture base; the acceptance
of any substance, natural or manufactured, as medium; and the
sculptural content springing from the artist's womanhood.

Traditional public sculpture rested securely on its formal elevated
pedestal, as you can see today in a stroll on Boston's Commonwealth
Avenue Mall. You will also see a work by **Penelope Jencks**, which
presents an alternative to the box base: a statue of historian Samuel
Eliot Morison casually perched on a large rock. Dressed in sailing gear,
he seems to look to the sea, imparting a sense of personality even to
those who know nothing of the man. It is the rock, however, that
begins this recognition.

In Jenck's Boston studio there are many works without pedestals,
sculpted from models: bathers sitting or lying and a series of imposing
female figures which gain veracity by their stance directly on the floor.
Jencks, always a serious figurative sculptor, developed a unique way of
working in life size terra cotta, eliminating the armature and building
up a hollow figure. When she began this in the sixties, both ceramists
and sculptors told her it couldn't be done. The figures are fired in a

special kiln in her studio.

Jencks feels that she could never make up anything as interesting as what she sees in the world. The gesture, slouch, resting of a hand, or twist of a foot is peculiar to a person. Yet, as she transfers these specifics to sculpture, the gesture is somehow no longer bound only to that actual moment and person, but becomes general body language.

A commission finished in 1984 reveals Jencks' searching eye. *Family* is in Promenade Park, Toledo, Ohio, an area descending from a mall to the river. Arriving by train on her first planning trip, Jencks noticed many family meetings and departures in the station. Walking around the site, she developed the clear idea of a family in the space. Differing from many outdoor figurative pieces, this family is not all grouped together. Mother is striding down the last few steps to the level of the other four. Father, holding an infant, leans against a cement area on which a small child squats to peer at something. Sitting almost 2000 feet away, at the edge of the water, a young girl dreams and gazes out across the river.

Thus the figures are placed naturally beside the users of the promenade and in echoing actions. Separating them sets up visual relationships tracing invisible lines among the group and within the extensive park area. Penelope Jencks successfully resists the tendency toward clustered figure groups which say, here is the art on this spot, separate from the world.

Marianna Pineda's sculpture has a very different spatial effect. A sculptor since the age of 17, Pineda lives in Boston, and has been exhibiting in major museum exhibitions for 38 years, with many commissioned works in public settings. She belongs with the traditional figurative sculptors, and one sees the influences of German Expressionists, modern dance, and medieval art in the smooth contours of her figures. But whatever formal inheritances there may be, content is personal and consistent. Images are evoked from womanhood and from a view of "women as authority figures, lovers, mourners, and dreamers." [1] Decades of strong work show women in joy or pain.

A recently finished life-size work, *The Defendant*, shows a woman in the dock, stooped in dejection, a victim over and over, now on trial.

Inspiration for the work came from a newspaper article and it symbolizes, "all the things that go wrong, fall on the woman." [2]

Contrasting with this private response is one of Pineda's major public commissions at the State Capitol in Honolulu. *The Spirit of Lili 'uokalani* is a bronze statue of the last monarch of Hawaii. Lili'uokalani was not only the Queen, but a spiritual leader believed descended from the sun, who is still revered. The standing figure is simply but eloquently presented. Her followers are very happy with the statue,which has become a religious shrine; people drape it with flowers and bow before it.

In each of these two very different sculptures, the subject is the spatial integrator. One sees *The Defendant* and empathetically enters into that body; one's head *is* that bent head. The spiritual content of Lili'uokalani pervades its area, and the space around it is activated by the movements of many people responding to a faith important to their lives. The modest space of the sculpture becomes a core for a greater meaning. Although rebuilding of ancient sites and celebratory structures by artists can have great visual power, without the impact of actual ritual use, they become areas bereft of the definition of the original. Pineda's work is an historical monument as well as religious art.

New rituals and celebrations are bringing opportunities for artists. In Boston the Bicentennial and the continuing First Night, Inc.[3] offer many of us the pleasure of doing large temporal work. **Ragnhild Reingardt-Karlstrom** of Brookline has made banners; giant fields of color which glow in light and define the day's air currents. Her largest was for Artpark in 1983. *Red Banner*, 65 feet long and 22 feet wide, suspended over a gorge, repeated the span of a bridge nearby. Holes in the banner for the wind provided additional color movement in the banner plane.

Using wind effectively is the essence of air art. Reingardt-Karlstrom plotted a new shape in a series called wind sculptures. The "Form-Reflections" are 24 to 30 feet in diameter as flat rings. Suspended from a guy line, they swell out when the wind enters one hole and leaves by the other. Filled, they are spherical, always moving, the light constantly changing, the sun coming through the top hole making a lively dot on the fabric. Strung at the World Trade Center, they were silhouetted alternately by the blue sky and the towers, light and shadows constantly forcing a perceptual realignment.

Sculpture in the air focuses on space within our daily purlieu, but somehow outside our ordinary concepts as though the power of gravity physically and pyschologically keeps us from fully using space and light. Now sculpture for and of the air appears more frequently in both evanescent and permanent work.

Joan Brigham came east from California. She saw steam sneaking out of manhole covers and billowing out of smokestacks on clear cold winter days and decided it could be used. Other artists have used steam occasionally, but Brigham is probably the first to use it successfully and continually as a sculptural medium and to develop an aesthetic for it.

Her first steam work was for the Boston Bicentennial in 1976, a Massachusetts Institute of Technology Center for Advanced Visual Studies project. This was followed by a series of collaborations with filmmaker Stan VanderBeek in which images were projected on steam. These works expanded to large narrative multimedia performances, collaborations with musicians, poets, dancers and other artists, presented nationally at festivals and museums.

Brigham's interest in steam has led also to smaller kinetic solar steam sculptures, about 4 x 4 feet. The series incorporates sun-heated black tubes and steam nozzles. In one, the steam power coming through two nozzles causes the unit to spin, forming a double helix.

Many of the large works have been participatory pieces in open spaces, which allow both overall views of the rolling, exuberant steam and close views in which the steam erases the world and enfolds you in its mystery. *Steamshuffle* was first presented in 1981 for the Cambridge River Festival and has been repeated at Boston City Hall and in Pittsburgh. Emmett Williams wrote concrete poems for it, which are etched on 8'x8' x 3/4" glass panels. The steam jets, on pipes running under the vertical panels, are independently activated when viewers intercept photocell beams. The random timing of obscuring steam clouds and the eventual evaporation to reveal the condensation of thought and water is accompanied by voices reading the poems through a sound system (developed by Chris Janney).

These pieces have been part of festivals and events where the audience is expectant and willing. Viewers can change the space, or groups can form spontaneously to "play" the billows, making the sculpture and space their own.

Brigham now has a permanent work in Cambridge. The Tanner Fountain was installed at the Science Center, Harvard University, in 1984 as the first combination steam and water fountain in the world. It is a collaboration with landscape architect, Peter Walker, who set five concentric circles of stone, and Robert Chaix, water consultant. The summer water and winter steam produce a similar, hovering mist above the inner circles of stones, so that there is a constant lively white cloud at eye level for people sitting on the outside stones or passing by. Visible for a distance, it is a presence urging one to closer observation, to catch the possible rainbow, or to watch the life of the steam, at once opaque and invisible.

Concentration on a transitory reality is also a factor in the work of **Harriet Casdin-Silver.** Casdin-Silver is a pioneer in holography, and her breakthroughs have made her preeminent in the field. She began in 1969 in a search for more sophisticated light for installations with chromed exhaust pipes, motion, sound, and light. Through Art and Technology, Inc., Boston's spinoff from New York City's Experiment in Art and Technology, she was offered the opportunity to work at American Optical Research Laboratory, which was curious to see what an artist would do. One of her first acts was something they had not considered. In early holography displays the plate was encountered first and the viewer moved beyond it to see the image. Casdin-Silver put the image in front, where it was more accessible. This encouraged her further experimentation to make the image project even further away from the plate.

Casdin-Silver's other firsts include using solar-trackers to employ the sun as the source for outdoor displays of holograms, and white-light-transmission art holograms. She has produced a host of holograms, including an installation using small multiple images of false teeth; a 6-foot horizontal head, *A Woman;* and multihued forks, part of a collaborative environmental project by the Center for Advanced Visual Studies, called *Centerbeam,* shown at Documenta '77 and the National Air and Space Museum.

For a performance in Montreal in 1985, Casdin-Silver created *Portail.* It began with dancers leading the audience through a ritual sequence around the chest-high plate and image. Then, with viewers on two sides of the room, the dancers moved through and around the image,which projected forward in a range of 30 feet. The use of space for a floating image separated from its source was magical. In a darkened area, with dancers circumscribing other moving images, the viewer must think about space anew. Unlike a mirage, the image is not insubstantial, but is suspended in matter invisible through our usual references. Sculpture, a tangible medium, increasingly becomes the realm of the conjurer.

The term "installation" used to mean one large work made for a specific area, using floor, walls, and ceiling. Those elements are totally transformed in installations by **Nancy Selvage.** She seemingly takes apart the given architectural structure and reassembles it into a complex, illusionistic environment of constantly confusing realities. Using scrim, screen, plexiglass, mirror, and wood, she manipulates perspective so that the space is altered in depth, walls are optically askew, and reflections and solid substance are ambiguous. You may see a mirror panel with its reflection path coming toward you, but upon moving closer you discover the path is painted on the floor and the panel is the reflection. In a long gallery area the floor seems to be an inclined plane, but only on the right side. How can this be? Selvage's installations are full of such mysteries, and they ask for an unhurried discovery. The intention is not illusion for its own sake, but to put us in a different state of mind.

Many of Selvage's spatial questions came from designing and building her own house. A builder constructs space for uses that may be unlike any former living situation, or even imagined functions. Will spaces built to dream specifications suit the realities of existence, or must we change our perceived reality to fit the space?

Critics are hard-put to describe Selvage's works, although their appreciation of the magic is clear enough. Like other camouflage, its production is based on clear thinking, in this case about our spatial perceptions.

Illusion is also important in my own work, which has to do with light and its effects: shadows, reflections, and color changes. In 1969, for a solo exhibition, I made 24 pieces for specific spaces or situations in the gallery, such as air currents, columns receiving light for a brief period daily, and corners. The sculptures were made of nylon net (a medium I have not seen used elsewhere), horsehair, or wire screening. Net, tulle,and maline enabled me to capture light three-dimensionally and to integrate shadow, sometimes ambiguously, as part of the sculpture. I have used net in geometric units, hanging from the ceiling, almost invisible in a corner, filling a room, or skimming along a floor. It allows sculptural volume to be evident, yet transparent, layers colors, and changes the way shadows define mass.

A 1980 installation, *Work for the Sun,* used seven Federal arched windows along one wall. Cut felt pieces the color of the sun spots were placed on the floor to match sun patterns at timed intervals for each window. Barely perceptible net stretched from the floor under the window at an angle to the ceiling. At each window the sun made a slanted window pattern on the glass, another one midair on the net, and another on the floor, which for a moment of its passage almost exactly covered the felt pane images.

In a 1983 commission, *Color Sweep*, for a public housing project in Needham, Massachusetts, I used light differently. Housing for the elderly and handicapped sits in a semicircular area. across the street from two gentle 9-foot high hills. On the other side, these hills slope down 25 feet to a level play area and backyards. I placed a row of posts to march up and over each hill, one in a north-south line, the other east-west, so that if continued to the lower level they would meet. These emphasize the rise and fall of the hills and connect the two housing clusters, with the swath of color a directional signal. Some part of the standing color can be seen from every section of the complex, although it is most visible from the elder's housing.

The posts, all painted the same, have one side red and the other three yellow at the top and blue on the bottom. The division is at a continuous angled line, so that the amount of each color reverses to its opposite side. In a line the colors all face the same way, and people see change as they walk by. Sometimes the colors they see are fleeting, perhaps not seen for another day or another season. This change is the result of color reflection from the sky and from one post to another. For example, the reflected red will change the blue gradually to violet and the yellow to gold. With a change in the sun's direction, blue may be the activator. At the end of a day the panels facing west can be seen as silver or gold in the fading light. Calculations for these effects included the course of the sun, the compass direction of the lines, positioning of the posts in the line, and the colors themselves.

I am engrossed by space as a container for light, seemingly invisible until we stop it, bounce it with a pinhead or wall, or use it to carve, define, cast, or mystify — at any distance.

An artist who presents sculptural still lifes without the human figure, **Mags Harries**, of Cambridge, has several public art works in the metropolitan Boston area. The earliest, *Asaroton*, (1976), is at Haymarket Square. Another, *Glove Cycle*, is in the Porter Square station on the MBTA Red Line. Before these, Harries worked with clay for years, seeking ways to depart from her classical training as a figurative sculptor, in which perfect form was content. She broke the whole into parts in both form and content and refitted the parts. In one series, she turned sections of women's bodies into environments. Casts of breasts, armpits, buttocks, and thighs became the sites of golf courses. beaches, and ski resorts.

Her attempt "to open up the realistic rendering of objects" [4] had another solution in the found object. Trash is already broken down, free of formal strictures, and natural scattering removes it from any sense of base. *Asaroton* is a prime example of the found object as collage. Leftover fruits, vegetables, and other residue of a day's outdoor market are cast in bronze. Imbedded in the streets at Haymarket, they mix with orange peels and squashed egg cartons. Time becomes another element, as shoppers, tourists, and vendors mash this week's tomatoes against the bronze corn, untrained performers in an endlessly repeated ritual. In *Glove Cycle*, made for a Cambridge subway stop, Harries again takes content and form beyond prescribed sculptural boundaries. 58 cast elements in the cycle are distributed singly and in groups on three levels. In preliminary planning, Harries moved through the space thinking "I am the public, I want an experience for myself to enjoy, and the public will too." [5] The experience includes surprise and humor. On one of several turnstiles, a glove holds a smaller glove, as if to receive your fare. On the strip between two escalators, new or scruffy gloves have been dropped, tumbled, and piled up, a few fallen to the floor. Walking to the platform, you spy others here and there. A woman's long dress glove and a man's winter glove point at each other in the *Creation of Adam* gesture. One is on the floor, by a bench, while in a far corner is a large pile, maybe two winters' worth, of mittens and gloves. Scattering throughout the station makes movement and time factors in realization of the whole work. Most sculpture uses space beyond its physical edges, and on occasion it seems palpable. In contrast, Harries' distribution of elements makes visible spots within thousands of travelers' individual paths. With sudden flashes or smoothly passing images, these objects enter our personal spaces and enliven them.

As sculpture has become part of the city square or subway system, the act of seeing it may range from a deliberate step forward to a casual glance in passing. Many glances from different directions during one's comings and goings may or may not add up to a thoughtful opinion. But these new opportunities also show how personal space in a public area can be appropriated by habitual use.

There are still gaps in knowledge about our sense of space: perceptually, emotionally, and physically. Perhaps some of the issues which emerge in environmental art will provoke research. In a sense, the artists discussed here are doing private research, but responding personally to questions about the space outside the sculptured object.

Notes:
1. From Marianna Pineda's "Artist's Statement," *Contemporary American Women Sculptors* by Virginia Watson-Jones. (Phoenix, Arizona: Oryx Press, 1986), p.46. Reprinted with permission from Oryx Press.
2. From a conversation with the author.
3. The city-wide New Year's Eve celebration of the arts in Boston was initiated by artists December 31, 1975. It begins in early afternoon with family events and ends at midnight with fireworks. There are both indoor and outdoor events: music, theater, dance, performance and environmental art, and a grand costume procession to join or watch.
4,5,&6. From a conversation with the author.

—**Virginia Gunter**

Virginia Gunter, Color Sweep (detail), 1983. Needham, Massachusetts.

Penelope Jencks, *Family* (detail), 1984.

WOMEN AND LANDSCAPE: INTERPRETING NATURE

*"One day I was walking along Tinker Creek thinking of
nothing at all and I saw the tree with the lights in it.
I saw the backyard cedar where the mourning doves roost
charged and transfigured, each cell buzzing with flame. I stood
on the grass with the lights in it, grass that was wholly fire,
utterly focused and utterly dreamed. It was less like seeing
than being for the first time seen, knocked breathless by a powerful glance. The flood of fire abated, but I'm still spending the
power... I had been my whole life a bell, and never knew it until
at that moment I was lifted and struck."*

— Annie Dillard [1]

At the age of twenty-nine **Roberta Paul** was known as one of
Boston's more original young portraitists. For five years she had
exhibited portraits, as well as figurative work and paintings of fish, and
was planning to continue in this vein. Then, in the spring of 1985,
she went to Brazil,where she took a short excursion into the Amazon.
She journeyed into the hot, humid, rain forest as an enthusiastic tourist,
an observer of exotic scenery. But when she left the forest two days
later it was as an insider, shaken to the bone, redirected, as it were, by
the visual spectacle and kinesthetic experience of the emerald kingdom.
Upon her return, Paul began to draw the lush vegetation of the Amazon
with a frenzied excitement, in an effort to capture on canvas, and to
relive, the intensity of her experience. Her serendipitous trip catapulted
her into a new stage of artistic production.

Paul is one of several women artists from the Boston area whose work
represents a natural world seen as though one were "thinking of nothing
at all," to use Annie Dillard's phrase. Their art rejects realist
objectivity and the tradition of *nature naturante* — nature as nature,
nothing more, nothing less— in favor of the subjective, intensely felt
personal response that has its origins in Romanticism. For all of these
artists, revelations in nature have come hand-in-hand with artistic
revelation and stylistic growth. Some, like Paul, have had intense,
dramatic experiences that affected their work immediately. Others,
attuned to nature from the beginning, reveal a steady enlargement of

vision over the years. This essay is about seven such women and the art they produced in the '80s.

Since Roberta Pauls' return from Brazil she has worked steadily on a series of large oilstick drawings entitled *Amazonas*, using stylistic devices invented to balance the inner drama of her experience with the outer reality of the forest. Each composition focuses on a segment of a particular type of vegetation, sometimes cropping part of it, sometimes placing a part just at the boundary of the framing edges. The latter device generates tremendous energy within the composition, for the vines, fonds, or leaves press hard against the borders, while at the same time they twist and turn in all directions. Paul applies her oilstick in heavy, quick strokes, as though it were oil paint, building it up everywhere in a thick, rich impasto. The intense energy level recalls the abstract gestural painting of Joan Mitchell, but the movement of Paul's hand is guided by a direct connection to the organic world. The solid dense pigment, particularly in the space surrounding the vegetation, suggests the heavy quality of the air, the almost palpable humidity of the forest. Lush green and yellow vegetation grows from a damp, dense claustrophobic space. We feel how the rain forest felt to Paul.

One of the most intriguing aspects of Paul's expressionism is her projection of human attributes onto objects in the landscape, an anthropomorphism which John Ruskin characterized as the "pathetic fallacy."[2] She presents the flora of the Amazon frontally and close up, as though they were sitters, and, indeed, they do seem to flaunt their remarkable, sensual features with a touch of the exhibitionist. In *Amazonas #10* (1985) in particular, Paul seems to transmute two trees into human beings. One is ovbiously male, the other female. Their roots are like legs, their upper branches like arms. They seem to dance together in wild abandon, recalling the figures in Emile Nolde's *Candle Dancers.*

Judith Berman for ten years explored a variety of the earth's creatures and their habitats, which then became subjects of monumental pastel and oilstick drawings. None of her expeditions affected her more powerfully than diving in the Carribbean, off Eleuthra (in the Bahamas) and off St. Martins and Anguilla (in the Leewards) in the early 1980s.

She found the experience of submersion in the ocean depths, of the freedom of weightlessness, of swimming alongside fish and sharing their habitat, enrapturing. This, combined with the spectacle at close range of the beauty and diversity of underwater life, affected Berman's art.

Her color, already rich, became spectacular. Her undersea worlds explode with color. *Comings and Goings I - Clear View* and *Songs of the Parrotfish* (both 1982) contain turquoise waters, yellow, chartreuse, and celery green corals, purple sponges, golden anemones, green, blue, orange, black, and white fish. While the color reflects what Berman actually saw, it also reflects the ecstasy and wonder she felt while under the sea. This use of color to celebrate the glories of the sensuous world brings Matisse to mind, especially his late cut-outs. But Berman's consistent focus on animal and vegetable life rather than on the human form cause us to ponder the marvels of a larger universe.

Like Paul, she interprets nature in an anthropomorphic way. In many of her studies of fish she emphasizes relationships between them, organizing them either in groups or head-to-head, where they appear to communicate. She encourages this reading in her titles, such as *Fish Games Too* (1983), *Hide and Seek* (1980), *Conversation* (1982), *Hey, What's Happening?* (1982) and *Sunday Afternoon* (1982), where two fish are about to begin a promenade in the water. An amateur naturalist, Berman has chosen to arouse our curiosity about these creatures rather than to represent them objectively. She reminds us that some things can never be explained by reason.

Elizabeth Awalt has for many years been inspired by elemental processes in nature. She is equally attracted by modest events, such as the growth of fiddleheads and skunk cabbages in early spring, or grand, dramatic events, such as the eruptions of a geyser or wholesale destruction of a forest by a volcano. Her powerful expressionist landscapes move and excite us.

In her paintings of forest enclosures, Awalt evinces her sense of the spirituality of nature, recalling the work of the Hudson River painters, particularly Asher B. Durand. Her *Warm Web* (1985), *At the Mercy of the Light* (1985), and *Light Nest* (1984), painted at the Yaddo art colony in upstate New York, bespeak the presence of the divine in nature. Light illuminates a dark forest interior; the space is sacred, a sanctuary. Her paintings of the Hoh Rainforest in Washington State explore the intense contrast between dark forest enclosure and the brilliant raking light of the sun.

When Awalt brings her intense focus to the harsher side of nature, she creates works that are poignant and haunting. In the northwest she was especially attracted to trees and the cruel fate, natural or otherwise, that often befell them — tree stumps amputated by the hand of man, trees blasted by the eruption of Mount St. Helens or killed by the heat of geysers, and redwoods with large burls, bulbous deformations that look like goiters. The tree or its remains may be in the foreground, forcing us to look at it before we look to the landscape beyond. Often the tree is human size, encouraging an anthropomorphic reading. *Death by Heat* (1985), for example, shows a tree in Yellowstone Park killed by the heat and sulfur of the surrounding hot springs. The branches have all broken off; the spiky remains read as the stumps of severed limbs. The bottom of the trunk is scorched white, the source of the nickname "bobbie socks" applied to such trees. The painting reads as a poignant metaphor for the human predicament in the nuclear age.

Anne Neely's work shares Awalt's intense vision of nature, especially trees, but Neely focuses exclusively on the pulsing life and energy of the natural world. Looking at Neely's oil paintings and what she calls her "spirit drawings," small preparatory oilstick sketches done on the site, one feels that she must live in a state of perpetual ecstasy, forever struck breathless by nature's glories. Whether she paints the mountains of the southwestern United States or the olive groves of Italy, she portrays a world pulsing with life. Her mountains seem to heave air, even to throb, as in *Out my Window* or *Over the Rise* (both 1985). Her trees, like Paul's, are almost humanoid, with "bodies" that bend like ours, with trunks that want to run or dance, and with branches like arms. One almost feels they speak, sing, howl, and chant when the lights are dimmed and we leave.

Neely sets brilliant colors one against another in unexpected combinations. In *Between the Cypresses* (1985), four trees with cool, light blue leaves stand in a fiery field of red and orange, chilling and

warming us at the same time. In *Four Cypress Trees* (1984-1985),
light yellow, red, blue, and green trees clash and blend. The expressive
colors recall both Munch and Van Gogh, but without their oppressive
overtones. She has learned much from their expressionism, and turned
it into a source of lyric beauty.

Marcia Lloyd's landscapes are as quiet and contemplative as Neely's
are noisy. Where the wind howls and leaves dance madly in Neely's
work, silence prevails in Lloyd's. Where brilliant hues appear in
startling, bold juxtapositions in Neely, Lloyd uses light greens and
blues of closely related tones that change almost imperceptibly. And
where Neely's paintings are charged with an electric energy, Lloyd finds
an inviolable quietude in the landscape of China, Ghana, Martha's
Vineyard, or the Blue Hills of Milton, Massachusetts. Whatever the
landscape, it is usually contained within a horizontal format, a structure
which furthers the sense of serenity.

Instead of projecting herself onto the landscape in identification with its
forms, Lloyd "empties" herself, letting go of associations and labels as
much as possible, in order, as she says, "to receive what is there to be
received." She eliminates most landmarks which establish associative
readings — individual trees, flowers, animals and birds — and takes a
more distant view. Typically, the elements are hills, gentle mountains,
screens of trees, and water, flowing together harmoniously in a unified
continuum. The one exception is in her Chinese landscapes, which
often include monasteries and temples, as in *Purple Cloud Paradise*
(1985) and *Tien Tie Shan* (1985), but these structures seem to belong
to the landscape, and facilitate meditation. Here, as in all Lloyd's
landscapes, we may wander visually, empty our minds, pause, reflect,
look inward, relax, daydream, or pray.

While Lloyd's meditative landscapes provide respite from the frenzy of
modern urban life, she herself, juggling two vocations, teaching,
painting, and living in South Boston, must work very hard to find quiet
time for her art. The peace and tranquility of her work are perhaps a
wistful corrective to the agitation and tempo of her life.

Liebe Coolidge and **Leslie Sills** both create child-like visions of
nature. Both maintain a distance from the pressures of careerism,
financial responsibility, and professional politics. Neither has travelled

extensively; both find inspiration in the landscape and nature around them, which they interpret with a wonderful freshness and innocence. Like the Douanier Rousseau, they transform the familiar into the strange and exotic.

Coolidge creates pastel and oilstick drawings of New England landscapes in which she freely distorts shapes, uses bizarre color combination and juxtaposes odd bits of reality to make us take a second glance at the world. In *Turtle Cove with Bacon Clouds* (1986), one of several studies of a quiet inlet in Cape Cod, Coolidge delineates a sunset with alternating black and pink lines resembling strips of bacon. In *Turtle Cove with Sausage Clouds* (1986), plump sausage links float in the sky. These odd yet beautiful skies, remind us of looking for familiar forms in the clouds as children. Coolidge also draws landscapes with animals, often her pets, including cats, dogs, a pig, a Jersey cow, a miniature mule, and a guinea hen. Typically these animals reside in tranquil settings. *Tonga Dreams* (1985) is an oilstick drawing of her Jack Russell terrier resting on a couch in front of a sky filled with cottony clouds. The dog gazes toward us, utterly relaxed and, it would appear, lost in a daydream. Coolidge makes us believe that reverie is within the realm of canine experience.

Since 1979, painter Leslie Sills has created a number of engaging small nature assemblages, most often inspired by a specific environment but bearing no direct resemblance to it. Rather, they evoke the magical quality that nature held for us when we were children and saw things for the first time. What did we feel the first time we walked into a forest enclosure? Enchantment with its beauty or a claustrophobic fear? What was our first experience of a beach? The immensity of sand, of ocean? Sills' little constructions help us recapture our original sense of wonder.

Through the extraordinary, often bizarre, juxtaposition of familiar and odd materials, man-made and natural, she surprises us with the unexpected. Her technique recalls Joseph Cornell, but acts on us differently. Sills frequently contrasts natural elements, such as bark and twigs, with synthetic materials, such as plastic jewels, as in *Nest Box* (1980) and *Nest Pod* (1985). Unlike much surrealist assemblage, the effect is not bizarre or enigmatic, but natural — the materials seem to belong together.

One of the most provocative and inventive devices Sills employs in her assemblages is a decisive separation between inside and outside: nearly all hide an interior world from view, while at the same time providing access to it. Frequently she closes off the view by a full or partial barrier. In *Whistling* (1986) and *The Dream* (1985), marvelous, miniature trees stand about two feet high, each with holes poked in its center, inviting us to come close and take a peek. Looking inside *Dream* we behold a forest of twigs and painted leaves, a gorilla, and a sleeping girl. What is happening? We do not know. In *Forest Primeval* (1985), a little enchanted forest is hidden within a clay and twig structure and we may imagine that this is the original primitive house from which all architecture evolved.

Sills' concepts of containment, enclosure, and concealment are "female" elements of which she is quite aware. In all these works she invites us to come close, to twist , bend, move, so we can behold the riches within the womb-like interior spaces. She helps us forget the normal distance we have learned to maintain between ourselves and objects. We reconnect momentarily with a former self, the child who once lived "thinking of nothing at all."

Notes:

1. Annie Dillard, *Pilgrim at Tinker Creek* (New York; Harper and Row, 1974), p.35.
2. John Ruskin, *Modern Painters* , III, eds. E. T. Cook and Alexander Wedderburn, *The Works of John Ruskin*, V (London; 1904), pp.201-220.

— **Bonnie Grad**

Liebe Coolidge, *Tonga Dreams,* 1985. Collection of Dr. Timothy Rivinus, Providence.

Judith Berman, *Hey What's Happening?* 1982.

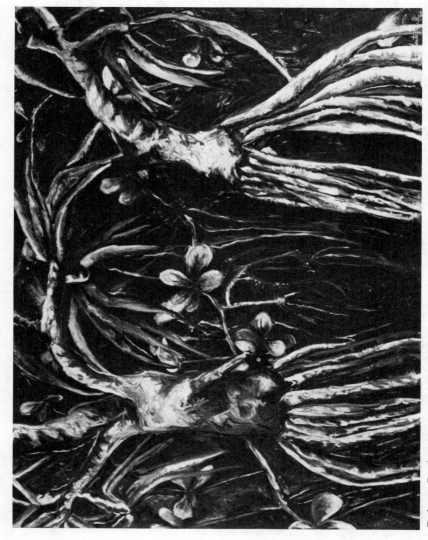

Roberta Paul, *Amazonas #10*, 1985.

INTERIOR SPACE
A DIALOG WITH THREE ARTISTS

One prevalent concern in the work of contemporary New England artists is interior space. Three Boston artists; Debra Weisberg, Liz Awalt, and Ruth Bauer work in very different modes, yet share this preoccupation. Weisberg uses soft materials, which she hardens to make wall constructions abstracted from natural forms. Awalt paints landscapes, tactile interpretations of places visited. Bauer paints mundane settings, lawns, houses, and gardens, but transforms them into mystical places which could be anywhere. Diverse in form and focus, the works retain interior space as subtext. Always searching for a psychological understanding of people and art, and having a personal interest in the use of interior space, I could not help but ask why.

The psychoanalytic world first began to deal with this issue in the 1930s. Freud thought that any objects enclosing a space or acting as pits, hollows, or caves were representations of female genitalia. He postulated that there were great psychological differences between men and women because of their physical differences, and that women would feel deficient and envious in not having a penis. Later Erik Erikson expanded Freud's theory by stating that the situation was more complex and maybe not so difficult for women. He theorized that woman's "inner space" counteracted her recognition that she is missing a penis. He thought that in order for her to develop the potential of her feminine psyche, she must accept "without apology" this inner space. Such acceptance would give her a sense of being sexually equal but different, be a basis for positive identification with her mother, and provide a sense of purpose arising from her ability to be (or become) productive — in other words, to bear children.[1]

What is irritating about these psychoanalytic views is, first, they limit one's perceptions not only of interior space, but also of how particular individuals may use it. Second, they embrace the power of the unconscious to such a degree that whatever one may say about why an artist uses interior space, another meaning — the genital/womb/mother interpretation — can be taken as the underlying reality.

But artists like Weisberg, Awalt, and Bauer represent an even more complicated reality, which Erikson's ideas cannot completely explain. This muliplicity of interpretation is necessary for my work as well.

My mixed-media constructions, often fetish-like objects or small-scale imaginary scenes, all share an enclosure, an interior space into which the viewer must sometimes literally project his or her head to see what's there. While the work does consciously deal with female sexuality and so makes clear reference to a vaginal iconography, that is just one level of meaning.

I've always found the connection of the female body to forms in nature, pods, flowers, seeds, sap, roots, and the like, significant. This is not to say that looking at a flower, for instance, reminds me of being a woman and so inspires me to represent one. In a more allusive way, being a female makes me feel spiritually connected to all that is alive and growing. However, phallic forms, also significantly abundant in nature, are just as prevalent in my work as vaginal forms.

Furthermore, the emotional component must be addressed. One might think that a preoccupation with a genitial view of nature could be only for the purpose of titillation or an expression of erotic longing. However, the myriad feelings we all exerience as humans, as animals that grow, change, and die, all have a sexual or sensual aspect. The sexuality becomes a filter, an attitude through which one can experience life.

The following are taken from interviews with Weisberg, Awalt, and Bauer, probing these particular issues. I wanted to find out why, if their main concern was not interior space, it was so obvious in their work, and what it meant to them.

Leslie Sills: I am constantly drawn in by your sculptures, yet at the same time equally aware of the outside. Do you think about this tension between an inside and an outside?
Debra Weisberg: I think about the inside and the outside simultaneously, and they're equally important to me. I work from the inside out. The process seems like simultaneous growth and disintegration. I begin with a sense of the outside shape, like a silhouette. The shapes start like an embryo and work their way out, evolving through a very slow process of layering. I see interior and exterior like the human body — the skin is just this layer, a thin,

Debra Weisberg, *Slow Burn*, 1985.

Elizabeth Awalt, Redwood Cave, 1986.

transparent layer, that stretches over a very developed form.

LS: Do you have a body identification with the forms?

DW: Yes. I think so. My pieces keep looking like my rib cage, tall as me and/or wide as me.

LS: Does this then imply that your forms are female?

DW: They are autobiographical in that sense, but I don't consciously create a female form. I think that I create my experience or my interior space, which is a female form. But the work is multi-leveled and complex. It feels like it's about creating, about birth. A lot of pieces have shells to them, and there is something inside coming to life. Or one might not be sure if it's decayed and what you are looking at are the remains. It is about the difference between degeneration and regeneration.

Leslie Sills: When I saw your recent work, I was struck by a number of paintings that focused on tree hollows. I have always thought of you as primarily a landscape painter, someone who goes outside and paints what she sees, even though I know you are selective. Yet for me, those hollowed- out trees seemed particularly provocative. Were you consciously aware of choosing these trees or did they just present themselves?

Liz Awalt: I did choose these particular trees because I was attracted to a shape, the shape that created a kind of interior space. So first it was the shape and later I started thinking of that shape as female. The tree itself seemed like a male form. My choice is based mostly on a direct response to those forms.

LS: Are you talking about erotic feelings?

LA: I don't think that those forms necessarily have to be sexual in terms of symbolism or meaning, but generally in nature, forms are erotic, as in the way things are hollowed out, the way natural forms die and go back into the earth. All these things seem to be erotic and therefore have a sexual quality.

In general, landscape painters either look at nature very objectively and see just what is out there, or look more subjectively and try to express how a certain space makes them feel, and then put that into the work.

LS: The interior space is really a metaphor for your emotional psychological interior?

LA: Yes, but it is also very real. There was a certain woods I painted a lot at Yaddo that gave me a feeling of walking into a place. The woods were very dark, as if they were a whole different time of day, even a different temperature from the rest of the area. The trees hovered above me making a canopy.

LS: You're saying it's a psychological /emotional statement but it's also a statement about a particular, physical place.

LA: Yes. But it is different in different woods. For instance, in the woods at Yaddo it was very dark, the color was very red and the light was very intense. However, in the rain forest on the West Coast, everything was very green, like an emerald forest, and very cool. Also, the size of the trees makes a difference. At Yaddo I walked into a space surrounded by the trees where I felt enclosed among them. In the rain forest the trees were so large that they towered over me.

LS: Yet the eroticism and connection to nature's life cycle comes through no matter where you are?

LA: Yes, it does.

Leslie Sills: When I saw your new paintings, I was drawn to the empty houses, which seemed to speak of isolation.

Ruth Bauer: The main themes of that series are isolation and barriers. There is always a fence, or trees, or shadows that act as barriers, real barriers or psychological barriers to impede movement into the painting. However, at the same time, I ask the viewer to move into the painting, usually with a path or lawn or an actual opening in a fence.

The houses are empty because they feel more mysterious that way. The windows are darkened so that they could be deep space that you reach into or flat space like a sheet keeping you out. The emptiness implies loneliness and isolation, and a mythic quality, as though one might be walking along, see this beautiful spot with an empty house, and wonder why it's empty.

The houses are symbolic of inner and outer feelings. Mainly I like to talk abut unseen things, about spiritual, psychological, and emotive themes, in my painting. I try to paint an inner reality.

LS: You are really identified with the houses.

RB: I don't think of myself as the house. I do think of it symbolically and there is an anthropomorphic quality, a sense of character. The windows are like eyes. I often emphasize that by putting in two windows. Also, the themes of loneliness and isolation are ones I've worked with a lot. And wanting to make a picture that people enter into has been important.

LS: Do you see this as female?

RB: I think that the stereotype of a woman artist is one who is concerned with spiritual, emotional, and psychological themes, and I do fit into that category. But men can have that in their work too.

It does seem that many women do artwork that relates to space. I'm obsessed with making interior spaces because they are symbolic of the emotive and spiritual themes I want.

LS: Do you see these houses as sexual symbols too?

RB: I tend to think in broad themes and sexuality is never far away. But I didn't make the paintings to be about a sexual experience.

LS: Do you feel there is an underlying eroticism in the work?

RB: I'm very concerned with making tactile paintings. They do have a sensual quality about them. That's also another way they draw you in.

LS: The houses also seem eerie.

RB: Yes. There is something eerie about them. I want them to have a sense of mystery, both compel you to come in and also frighten you.

LS: Is that how you feel about people?

RB: Yes. I guess I do feel that way about relationships, too. That's why there are barriers in the paintings. I think of myself as a quiet person and so the paintings are understated. I prefer subtlety; I like ambiguity. I like people to look at them and not know immediately what they are about. I like to have them unfold and mean different things at different times, open-ended.

LS: Your paintings are of Salem. So would you say that being in New England is important for your work?

RB: Yes. I have a hard time imagining living elsewhere. What's intriguing to me about Salem is its sense of history, layers of history and experience. There is really a sense of decaying elegance, of living and dying at the same time, like Venice. The houses have an anthropomorphic sense to them. They are unique but crumbling. Then there are all these astonishing gardens that are so luxuriant but unkempt, also giving an eerie sense of living and dying.

Did you see the graveyard I have right outside? It's very beautiful, very peaceful, the oldest in Salem. We look out on it, so when I get up in the morning that's the first thing that I see. The tombstones are a constant reminder of what's there, what's there in life.

One can see that these women are all representing themselves. Their work is very personal, and identified with the life cycle, but not in easily defined ways. The spiritual seems a significant element, but so does the physical world. To define interior space for them as solely a female/womb image, even having Eriksonian ramifications, is a mistake. Interior space is representative of their internal life and not necessarily with female-only attributes. Perhaps Jean Arp was aware of this fluidity between the creative woman and man and nature when he said,

"Art is a fruit that grows in man, like a fruit on a plant or like a child in its mother's womb."[2]

Notes:
1. Carol E. Franzt and Kathleen M. White, " Individuation and Attachment in Personality Development: Extending Erikson's Theory," *Journal of Personality*, (June 1985), p.229.
2. Whitney Chadwick, *Women Artists and the Surrealist Movement.*, (Boston: Little Brown, 1985), p. 142.

—**Leslie Sills**

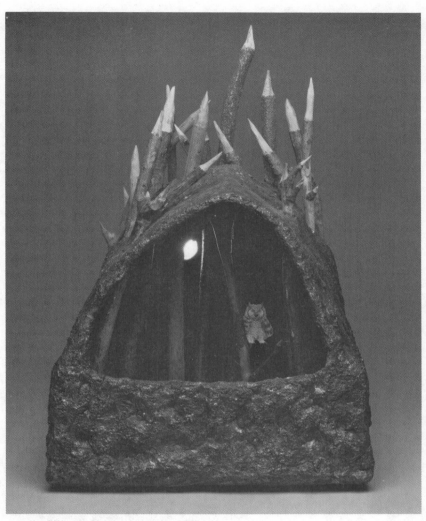

Leslie Sills, *Forest Primeval*, 1985.

Ruth Bauer, *Looking Out*, 1986.

COLLAGE: WHEN THE MARGINS ——— BECOME THE CENTER ———

Writers struggling to characterize the contemporary cultural landscape have often described a shift away from, or break with, modernism, and have labeled this trend "Postmodernism." Where modernist artists have been described as seeking centrality and authenticity, with the art work acting as a kind of esthetic whirlpool, the postmodern situation is seen as being so radically decentralized and fragmented as to deny any focus or sense of concentration. Even the primary role of the artist is denied; authorship, originality, coherent causal chains of production and reception are all disrupted. The locus of meaning of the work of art is not to be found in the work; rather, it is dispersed among its viewers. The gears have been thrown into reverse; centripetal glue is replaced by centrifugal dispersal, and the esthetic whirlpool is spun out into its diverse, vast audience.

In terms of sequence, some writers argue that modernism was dominant until the late 1960s, at which point its exhausted forms were broken up into the postmodernist esthetic. Others argue that modernist works have coexisted with their opposite as a kind of anti-modernism since early in the century. In terms of value, however clearly the faults of modernism are described, no writer is particularly sanguine about postmoderism. When all the world seems made of fragments spinning by us too fast to grasp; when the piece's original shape was in fact never original but only a copy of something never itself pretending to be authentic; when, in short, the mass-media-saturated urban consumer environment is their primary landscape, most writers seem edgy — euphoric or giddy at best, but never sanguine. There is, however, another way of looking at all this. Against this edginess, against this concern with the rupture and dispersal of modernism's focused concentration, stands a body of work that has always dealt with fragments as if they were the only coinage, the only commerce of perception: women's collages. To be sure, many women use collage as a way of making artworks, and not all of them privilege the fragment. Soon after the most recent women's movement gained momentum, many collages seemed to have been built with the assumption that shared gender would provide a pool of common experience to which all materials in the collage might refer, a pool that all the artists could treat as a common bank of meaning. That assured, the luxurious materiality of a dance card next to a satin ribbon, the sensuous formal contrast of a bit of lace next to a feather, would invoke the shared essence of the female gender. These collages were, in short, just another whirlpool.

When more emphasis is placed on the socially constructed nature of gender, however, such a shared essence is less easy to assume, less reliable as a bank of meaning. There is another group of collages that seem to have been made under different assumptions; the preliminary rhetorical choice of the women making them seems to have been to use fragments, not as signposts in a charted, occupied territory, but because the fragment itself — the caught glimpse, the partial view, the interrupted task, the obstructed gaze — was the primary existence of the artist. These artists' strategies for construction were always to assemble, to collect, to weave, to piece. What is impressive, inescapable, in fact, about these collages is the diversity of their materials. The work of four women who live and work in and near Boston embodies this diversity, and includes a broad spectrum of materials.

The work of **Maud Morgan** constitutes one point on this spectrum. No collage is purer, more abstract than hers. That is, the information her materials bring to the collage is nearly always formal; they are not interesting because of any meaning they might have in another context. I know only a very few of her collages that include photographs, for example. Her first, *Burlap Collage* (1958) consists of very similar, small pieces of burlap with frayed edges blending into a painted canvas ground. Morgan's earlier work was in painting and various printmaking techniques; her subsequent work in collage proceeded in fits and starts; she eventually used scraps of a destroyed painting, scraps of color-aid paper, Japanese mulberry and rice papers, and, later, handmade papers.

The ground rules of Morgan's collage compositions seem to have been transferred directly from her abstract painting and read, in fact, as part of a long, complex conversation about color composition carried on by such painters as Hans Hoffman (in the figure-ground color relationships in his rectangle paintings) or Mark Rothko (in the attention to the dissolving edge). And at first look, Morgan's collages seem very much all of a fabric, with an insistence on a unified surface. In *Burlap Collage*, for example, unraveled edges of burlap all but blend into the atmospheric painted ground. The later paper collages are sometimes glued, but are often composed while wet so that the paper fibers blend. Ultimately, however, a process of comparision begins, and pieces which had seemed similar outside the conditions of the collage can be scrutinized in the controlled circumstances of the work. In the paper collages, edges, differences, are held onto, as if illustrating the various formal conditions under which specific, separate things can get along in a crowd.

The manner in which painted, illusionistic space can serve as a kind of foil for actual, physical space, throwing even the flattest of materials into relief, provides **Claudine Bing** with a formal means to explore time and space. In her collages, painted space alternates and is layered with relief materials. Bing sees her collages as a way of thinking about a given physical space and all the things that have happened in that space, forms of life that have passed through it, configurations of physical arrangements that have crowded and emptied it, and messages that have filled its air.

Several kinds or sets of spaces are explored in her work, none of them literal rooms or landscapes. One set could be called diaries/letters/messages, another the art institution/gallery/museum, a third the moumental historical site. The first set, *Letters to Myself*, (1980), explored the shapes an envelope can be, enclosing to hide and opening to reveal secrets in hardly legible writing, as well as bits, of drawings and paintings. A series of very small collages, (also 1980) was based on scraps of napkins from the National Gallery of Art, the disposable remnants of consumption in the purported temple of the permanent. Bing's later *Monument* series is a group of much larger works that seem at first glance to be paintings, until one notices the surfaces sliding down past the framing edge. Indeed, the Monuments look like compost heaps of space, slung vertically. Inspired by visits to monuments in Greece and Mexico, they represent the space of another time and place, a world in which there is no pretense of ever seeing the whole thing. Bing has said that she wants things in her collages to look familiar, but not recognizable, and that sense of halted recognition, of always only seeing part of what is or has been, of time rushing through space, is the theme of her work.

The sense of a specific, recognizable place is very strong in the collages of **Marilyn Pappas**. They cohere around material from a certain place, especially what a traveler or visitor might handle — maps, receipts, labels, guidebook, illustrations. Pencils, oil crayons, and oil paint sketch a further map of the place. Views often flip perspective: in *La Grand Canyon du Verdun est Sauvage* (1979), a map of the southern coast of France with the canyon marked on it occupies the bottom of the picture, while a view of the mountain range seen from the bottom of the canyon is drawn and pasted in paper above. The emotional landscape is included as well; the festive mood and holiday nature of the trips are evoked in ribbons, drawn and actual, floating above the tops of several collages. Pappas says the illusionary interior decoration of Italian churches, with their painted marble and stucco ribbons, intrigued her. The movement back and forth between artificial and real, drawn and actual, is never sharp in these collages. It is rather a slide, a hybridization, a merging of separate phases of reality.

In large collages on paper Pappas represents Rome. The slippage in these is dizzying; flat maps alternate with bird's-eye views, Roman marble gods are replaced by baroque saints, which in turn give way to contemporary billboards. In most, maps dominate enough to serve as a convention for looking, plotting, and orienting oneself in the landscape, a convention undercut as soon as one's eye moves to left or right. For all the evocation of mood, however, there is very little focused emotion, and certainly little nostalgia for the glorious past of places visited in Greece, Rome, Egypt, and Mexico. The monuments of the past are major in the work, since they are the reason for the visit and for the collage, but the immediate sensory environment of the present is always at least as vivid, so a forceful leveling of perception occurs. The total of all experiences at each site is suggested, with no hierarchy of importance distinguishing single moments or specific views.

The collages of **Rosamond Wolff Purcell** are unusual in this group in that they themselves are rarely exhibited; one almost always sees them as large (20"x24") Polaroid color photographs, shiny and smooth (which classifies them as montages, according to some). One of

Marilyn Pappas, *Roma, Roma, Roma*.

Claudine Bing, *The Shaping of Monuments, 2*, 1983

Purcell's favorite stories is *The Book of Sand*, by Jorge Luis Borges, in which the author describes a large heavy volume that opens to an infinite number of pages, none of which can ever be relocated. "Permanent on the shelf, but impermanent as soon as you open it," is the way Purcell describes it, and this could describe her photos of collages as well. The collages themselves are striking in two respects. First, they have an air of material luxury; they are packed full of fascinating detail, crowded with remarkable objects, glittering slightly in dark, rich profusion, reminding one of cluttered, elaborate cabinets and walls of fanatic collectors or whole civilizations in crystal on top of a dressing table. Second, the collages are often built into windows, leading one to look through them as if into nature, into the natural order of things. Both impressions are highly misleading.

The stuff of which the collages are made is the stuff a collector would discard, and there is nothing natural about it. Almost nothing in the collages is original or unique or valuable. There are book illustrations, old photographs, paperback novel texts, newspaper magazine covers — or rather, there are bits of all these things. Nothing is in mint condition. The materials are in shreds, bits, fragments, and many are stained or foxed by mold. Nearly everything was mass-produced, nothing passed the test of time to become famous, and all is refuse, in poor condition. As one of Purcell's titles suggests, all was manufactured for, distributed into, and forgotten by *The Public Domain*. These assembled materials with histories are far removed from the purity of Maud Morgan's collages. The windows do not lead one to look into nature, but are packed full of culture, their initial, sensational come-on unravelled, ruptured, stalled.

The very wide range of materials used by these four artists does form a spectrum, from the traditional esthetic materials and abstract orders of Maud Morgan to the gathered refuse and specific references of Rosamond Purcell, moving from the studio to the streets, from the pure to the polluted. Nevertheless, these women also, finally, share a certain similarity of working method and compositional practice that might be seen as constituting a genuine difference in women's collage. From the intelligent spirit of compromise in Maud Morgan's paper collages to the halted recognition informing Claudine Bing's painted wall reliefs, from the multiple vantage points of Marilyn Pappas's site-maps, to the damaged goods and rifled spaces of Rosamond Wolff Purcell's photographs, there is a sense of fragmented, heightened perception, of always having more than one thing in mind or in sight.

There are obvious reasons; experience has led them to it. Marilyn Pappas says she has never in her life known anything but multiple roles, multiple identities. She always has had her mind simultaneously on art-making, teaching, and family. Claudine Bing points to the advantages of collage when you are certain your work will be interrupted; the hours of focused concentration needed to paint with oil, let alone do something like pour bronze, were not hers.

Focused concentration is replaced by a heightened perception in the conditions of distraction. Because no unified, concentrated span of time was available, no single coherent order is established, although the existence of such orders is recognized. All four artists often build up a false approximation of a received way of looking — the conventions of abstract painting, the private journal, the map, the window — and then treat this way of looking almost like a found object, calling the assumptions on which these patterns of sight rest into question by the very way in which they are physically rebuilt. The composite, the compromise, the comprehensive, including the husks of given modes, constitute a different order of perception, one part of the socially built character of many women.

One speculates that this order is shared by many who have found themselves on the margins of society, for whom long hours of self-directed work were never possible, for whom single points of view were not comprehensive enough, for whom the map or the window was always shifting in mid-gaze, for whom work was perpetually changing in mid-construction. Perhaps the conditions of postmodernism are the conditions of marginalism experienced by many women all along; for better or worse, the rest of our society now finds itself sharing their position. For these women, the dissolution of modernism is no tragedy, since it never expressed their experience. They have been occcupied all along with a different way of seeing.

—Johanna Gill

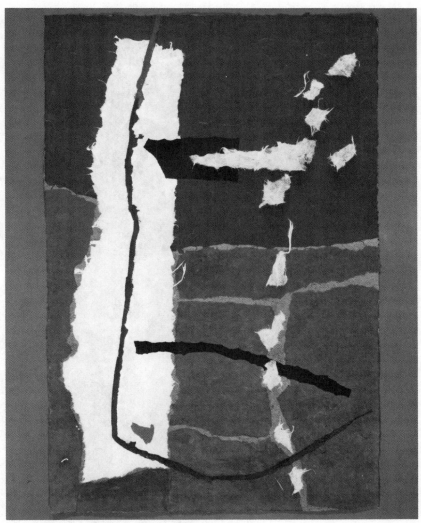

Maud Morgan, *Collage #210*, 1981.

Ilse Getz, *Ninth Avenue Window*, 1965. Courtesy Alex Rosenberg Gallery, NY

The Sunday *New York Times* Connecticut section reviews one major exhibition each week and competition for that review is great — which is often proclaimed to be a healthy and challenging situation. There are in addition a great wealth of opportunities available to artists in Connecticut, a great many of whom are women. The number of art exhibits listed each week in calendars of events in newspapers and magazines is truly impressive.

Connecticut artists, however, do have a close relationship geographically and aesthetically with the New York City museum and gallery scene. Many are close enough to readily attend museum blockbusters and gallery exhibits and to follow closely art criticism pertaining thereto. This, on the one hand, is a valuable asset for inspiration and exposure to new trends (and hype), but on the other, it can result in over-influence by fashionable trends.

While Connecticut artists do thus benefit from the New York art scene, it is difficult to get New York curators and gallery people to come to Connecticut. In fact they tend to fly to California, Chicago or St. Louis before going to nearby Hartford or New Haven.

Why then does a serious artist live in Connecticut? Many simply cannot afford to live in New York, but get along well in Connecticut with a teaching job, or other art-related position. Much more space per dollar is available in which to work, raise children, and pursue family life, and there is, of course, the added benefit of nature and the New England outdoors.

Some artists have such formidable talent that they can have one-person exhibitions in both Connecticut and New York. Foremost among these is Helen Frankenthaler, who for many years has shared both locales, as well as exhibiting throughout the world in virtually all major museums. Others who have in somewhat the same manner established respected reputations are Ilse Getz, Anni Albers, Sally Hazelet Drummond, photographer Barbara Morgan, and sculptor Rhys Caparn.

Several artists who live, work, and exhibit in Connecticut also are represented by New York City art galleries and have received critical acclaim. Among them are painters Alberta Cifolelli, Carol Anthony, Nancy Ketchman, Carol Unger, Martha Reinken, Jacqueline Gourevitch, Lucy Sallick, painter-printmaker Ann Chernow, and sculptors Carol Kreeger Davidson, Shaw Stuart, and Jean Woodham.

Younger artists who are beginning to receive special attention as talents to watch: painters Stephanie Adam, Karen Santry, Deborah Muirhead, Melody Fiore, Christy Gallagher, and sculptors Rachel Berwick, Beverly Fishman, Deborah Frizzell, Jane Morse, and Joy Brown.

Other distinguished Connecticut artists include Eve Ingalls, Shirley Kraus, Margaret McKinnick, Carolyn Rugen, Francine Funke, Rita Edelman, Barbara Rothenberg, Carol Dixon, Janet Mass Satz, Bonnie Woit, Maggie McCurdy Maureen McCabe, Susan Reinhardt, Nancy Lasar, Margaret Stekla, Jane Hall, Lucille Grimm, Elizabeth Bart, Priscilla Roberts, Irene Neal, Lucy Baker, Cookie Finn, Lou Hicks, Adele Hammond, Juliet Holland, Enid Monroe, Redenta Soprano, Helene Brier, Connie Kiermaier, Anna Held Audette, Judy Dolnick, Barbara Gray, Sophie Acheson, Jan Sutherland, Leona Pierce, Carol Eisner, Elizabeth McDonald, Jay Wulke, and Jane Willoughby.

There are also fiber artists Dolly Curtis, Norma Minkowitz, Irene Reed and Marlene Siff, papermakers Helen Frost Way, Phyllis Peckar, and Peggy Schiffer, and photographers Wilma Ervin, Eva Fuka, Inge Morath, and Renata Ponsold. Sculptors building reputations are Joyce Rappaport, Ruth Dyer, Joanna Beall, Tina Logan, Judith Kahn Steinberg, Jane Trask, Ruth Gutt, Timmie Ogden, Vera Schupack, and Jill Disque.

Many Connecticut museums and curators exert special efforts to showcase developing Connecticut artists. These include the Housatonic Museum of Art (David Kintzler); the Bridgeport Museum of Art, Science and Industry (Evalyn Milman); the Bruce Museum, Greenwich (Nancy Hall-Duncan); Old State House, Hartford (Joseph S. McLaughlin); Matrix Gallery of the Wadsworth Atheneum ("America's oldest museum"), Hartford (Andrea Miller-Keller); the New Britain Museum of American Art (Daniel Dubois); the Lyman Allyn Museum, New London (Dr. Edgar de Mayhew); the Mattatuck

Museum, Waterbury (Ann Smith); and the Stamford Musem & Nature Center, Art/Ex Gallery (Dorothy Mayhall).

There are also a wide variety of arts organizations across the state. Among the most active and supportive are Farmington Valley Arts Center; Bridgeport Art League; Greenwich Art Society; Silvermine Guild, New Canaan; New Haven Paint and Clay Club; Lyme Art Association; Washington Art Association; New Canaan Arts Society; Stamford Art Association; Stamford Community Arts Council; and the Weston-Westport Arts Council.

On a less optimistic note, a major exhibition of women artists, "American Art: American Women 1965 through 1985," held at the Stamford Museum & Nature Center in early 1986, included only three Connecticut women out of a total of 60 artists. All but four exhibitors were New York based. These statistics were about the same for a 1971 exhibition, "26 Women," held at the Aldrich Museum of Contemporary Art in Ridgefield.

While an artist might consider herself a "Maine artist," or a "Boston artist," the identity of "Connecticut artist" is much weaker. Connecticut as a regional entity in art has not developed to the same extent as in other New England states, largely due to the proximity of New York City. The New York-Connecticut border is sufficiently vague or porous that, for many artists and curators, it can be imaginary. Despite this and its comparatively small size, Connecticut stakes a legitimate claim to being one of the major states in terms of support and promotion of the visual arts, as well as proportion of artists in the general population.

—**Dorothy Mayhall**

Deborah Frizzell, *Fallen Limestone*, The Connecticut Gallery, Marlborough, Connecticut.

Ann Chernow, *Ten Cents a Dance*, 1984. Courtesy Armstrong Gallery, NY

Joan Curtis, *Kundrie*, 1985.

A group of women artists who are residents of Vermont by birth or inclination have been exceptionally active in bringing their work to the public and in the process sweeping away any residue of bucolic imagery. Inventive constructions, environmental sculpture, or dynamic mixed media work are what you will find coming out of Vermont women's studios these days.

Though it arrived in Vermont somewhat late, the women's art movement has had a strong impact. An active art community now exhibits in such centers as Burlington, Montpelier, Rutland, Brattleboro, Manchester, and Woodstock. Largely through the efforts of the Vermont chapter of the Women's Caucus for Art, opportunities for women's exhibitions have increased in the state's galleries and museums. The chapter also sponsors its own annual shows, and several artists have participated in group shows outside the state, such as at A.I.R. and Pindar Galleries in New York City in 1986. The chapter hosted the 1985 Northeast Regional Conference of WCA, and in 1986 honored women of the region, such as gallery owners and teachers, for their support of women's art.

There have been other signs of feminist consciousness in art. A seminal exhibition, organized in 1982 at the Brattleboro Museum by artist **Nancy Storrow**, called *Women's Art/ Women's Lives,* presented work by 19 women then living in Vermont. In conjunction, an historical exhibit, *Indomitable Vermont Women,* dealt with the role of the state's women from 1800 through 1920.

Storrow wanted "to show other artists and the public at large what Vermont women artists were doing." What they were doing, she believed, was "excellent work . . . making significant contributions to the already rich cultural heritage of our state."[1] Included were such varied pieces as photo collages by **Terry Gips**, terra cottas by **Melinda White**, a polychromed constructionist sculpture by **Meg Walker**, and performance pieces by Meredith Monk.

The T. W. Wood Gallery at Vermont College in Montpelier, under the directorship of Mary Ellen Martin, is one of several institutions that have encouraged women's exhibitions and sponsored seminars, readings, and other events. In November, 1986, for example, an exhibition titled "Four Women" presented the nontraditional work of **Mary Admasian, Aurore Chabot, Joelen Mulvaney**, and **Grace Grasmere Schust** (a New Hampshire Artist). Admasian's and Schust's massive semiabstract acrylics, Chabot's ceramic sculptures and geometric paintings, and Mulvaney's oils impressed critics as "unexpected and provocative" [2] and "challenging."[3]

In 1985, a collaboration between Vermont women poets and visual artists opened at three galleries in Burlington, curated by **Mary Ann Ricketson**. Part of the show traveled to Smith College in Northampton, Massachusetts, and to the Catamount Film and Art Center in St. Johnsbury, Vermont, followed by an exhibition of the entire 21 works at Montpelier's Wood Gallery.

The visual artists involved were all members of the Vermont Women's Caucus for Art, who worked over a two-year period with area poets. A total of 30 women took part in the intimate exploration of work and image relationships, creating such intriguing juxtapositions as Meg Walker's mixed-media *A Passage Tomb,* a stark white mausoleum accompanying **Judith Yarnall**'s multipartite poem, "Who Lives Under the Hill?"; and *Kundrie* (Parsifal's Grail Maiden), the colorful, awe-inspiring papier maché construction with moving parts that **Joan Curtis** dreamed up to complement **Marianne Lust**'s richly textured poem.

Dealing with everything from the mundane ("Hanging the Wash") to the archetypical ("Universal Women"), with a three-minute animated film by **Nancy Stone** to the accompaniment of a reading of "Order into Chaos" by **Kathleen Willard**, the collaboration exemplifies the diversity, creativity, and ingenuity of the energetic women of Vermont. Through their talents and efforts, Vermont art today is not all birches and sugar maples.

Notes:
1. Noel Suter, *Art/New England*, (October, 1982).
2. Lilli Lenz, The Barre-Montpelier *Times Argus,* (November 4, 1986).
3. Kathy Miller, *The Vanguard Press,* Montpelier, (November 2-9, 1986).

— Sylvia Moore

Meg Walker, *Who Lives Under the Hill*, 1985.

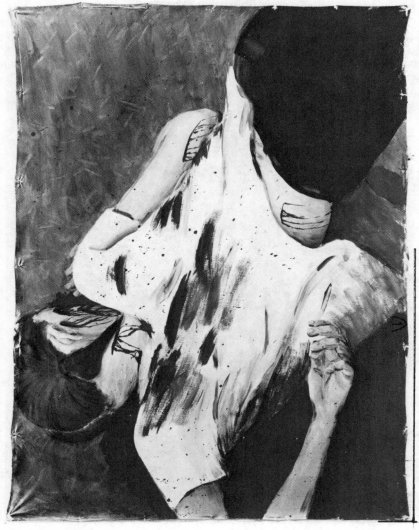

Linda Elwood, *She Asked for It Series I-IV,* 1984.

"POLITICAL" ART
BY NEW ENGLAND WOMEN

There are relatively few women artists in New England doing politically inspired work, and even fewer who are well-known. When I contacted museum curators in Maine, Vermont, New Hampshire, Connecticut, and Massachusetts, few could supply information, and some could not come up with a single name. One curator was not even aware that her museum was exhibiting work that dealt with sexual politics. However, I spoke with some local critics and gallery people who were most helpful and knowledgable. One gallery in Boston deserves special mention because it represents four women artists, whose work has a political content. The Stux Gallery on Newbury Street represents Judy Haberl, Jod Lourie, Susan Morrison, and Gina Fiedel.

Frustrated by this dearth of information, I sent a mailing to members of the Women's Caucus for Art in the New England states. Since I live in Boston, most of my information pertained to Massachusetts. The mailing helped adjust the balance, and I found a number of women doing very intriguing work.[1] I focus here on artists with whom I am most famiiar, and those not already well known to the public. One reason for writing this article was that my own paintings have political content, and sometimes I've felt myself working in a vacuum. It was delightful to meet others with similar concerns

Originally, my own work attempted to explore human character through line, form, and stroke, generally using oil paint on paper. Then I saw an article in the June 25, 1983 *Boston Globe* that described the trial of one Clarence Burns, who shot his wife Patti five times in the face, killing her. In June of the following year Judge Alvin Lichtenstein sentenced Mr. Burns to a two-year term in the Denver County Jail for his crime. "The sentence permits Burns to serve his jail term at night only, while continuing to work as a meat cutter. Judge Lichtenstein said in passing the sentence that Mrs. Burns may have provoked her husband by leaving him without warning." Mr. Burns had a long history of brutalizing his wife.

This article led me to create a series of paintings called *She Asked for It* — a series which now has three parts. Like other artists whose work is described on the following pages, I had come to realize that it was impossible to separate myself and my work from the world around me. If my work was to deal with human character, stylistically and thematically, I knew I had to investigate all aspects of character, even the most painful ones. I have tried to use the human figure as an emotionally charged vehicle, while simultaneously exploring the expressive qualities of line and stroke.

The three parts of the *She Asked For It* series focus on how violence affects women. Many people find the subject and the way I handle it unsettling, so I have difficulty getting the work shown. The first part of the series is based on real people and events described in news media (horrifying documents, the daily papers— at least from a woman's perspective). These are large (45"x54" to 70"x90") acrylic paintings on canvas. The second part of the series consists of large (70"x60") oil-on-canvas portraits of women, concentrating on their faces. The third part explores the personality schism women must undergo to survive in this most imperfect world. I see my concerns mirrored in the work of other women living in New England.

Maine artist **Natasha Mayers'** art is actively political, using drawing, painting, and assemblage to express concern about oppression. Mayers went to Nicaragua for three weeks in 1984 with the Artists' Brigade to work on a mural at the Prego Soap Factory. The experience changed her art considerably, because she discovered a whole new realm of function for art. "There are centers for popular culture everywhere in Nicaragua. Art can enable people to imagine action," she said. "Artists discover they have work to do in the world." Mayers, who believes art can be both aesthetically and socially effective, is an art therapist with psychiatrically disabled people, an activity that has strongly influenced her art. She feels a childlike and more freely expressive and witty character has developed in her work through this contact.

New Hampshire artist **Jeanne Lachance** says of herself, "I am a strong, independent woman. I've been alone twelve years and brought up four children." Her prismacolor drawings are sensitively rendered but disturbingly confrontational, dealing with all manifestations of sexual politics. Lachance says the works have their roots in pain. *Hera's Hanging* represents suicide. *Aphrodite's Anguish* tells of child abuse.

Parts of things are used to represent the whole, as in a three-painting sequence Lachance calls her "Woman Series," in which vintage blouses represent three women— "one empty, one trapped, one proud." (Staci Mibouer, *Sunday Telegraph*, May 25, 1986.)

Marcy Hermansader is a graduate of the Philadelphia College of Art who has been living in Vermont for several years. Hermansader works primarily with prismacolor pencils, making rich, visually complex drawings. She sent the following in a statement about her work:

I do not think of myself as a political artist, but since the mid-seventies about a third of my work could be put in that category. These subjects sprang quite naturally from events in my life— being a volunteer in the Women's Crisis Center, working in a factory with toxic chemicals, or simply reading the newspaper. The feminist slogan, "the personal is political" comes to mind. In my life and in my work I slide quite easily between them.

 Mimi Love feels that Vermont artists have an opportunity to produce political art by working through peace organizations. She donated her "Peace Banner for the Earth" to Artists for Social Responsibility. Made for the annual "Gathering for Justice and Peace" sponsored by Artists for Social Responsibility, Physicians for Social Responsibility, and Parents and Teachers for Social Responsiblility, the banner aimed "to show the effects of hunger or nuclear proliferation on life as we know it."

Love had been involved in several other peace projects. One was the Ribbon Project— an 18"x36" banner with peace ribbons from each state brought to Washington, DC for the fortieth anniversary of the Hiroshima and Nagasaki bombings. The subject was what you would like least to lose in a nuclear holocaust. At her son's suggestion, Love's choice was Spring.

Margaret Plaganis is another artist who feels an artist's philosophy should be included in her work. She says, "art doesn't happen in a sterile environment." Currently living in Connecticut, Plaganis is active in the Connecticut Women's Caucus for Art. A mixed-media artist, she admits no limitations on materials for her assemblages and constructions, but, "People don't know what to do with my work. They don't know how to classify it." It is controversial and has provoked some sharp reactions. She told me it's both "intensely personal and broadly archetypal," dealing with "the currents of the artist as well as the currents of the culture." Concerned with functioning in society as a person and as an artist, Plaganis does not separate the two.

Susan Schwalb, relocated in Boston from New York City, has a long history of feminist activism. She explained that, having grown up with no women artist role models, she wondered, "How can I be an artist if I am a woman?" Through the women's movement she gained an understanding of her difficulty in feeling legitimate as an artist.

Schwalb makes sensitive, strong, very personal silverpoint drawings on paper. These originally dealt with sexual imagery, although not in a realist manner. An earlier body of work had quite graphic vaginal imagery, but now the drawings are more abstract. Themes are sexual politics, religion, and memories of ancient civilizations, though, Schwalb is quick to add, her pieces are not intended to be Icons or Goddesses. She feels uncomfortable categorizing her work. "Labels cut people off from art," she says. She comments also that she finds the Boston art scene very different from New York's, and in some ways not as conducive to controversial political statements.

Photography seems the exception to any lack of enthusiasm for political art in Boston. **Bonnie Donohue** says she is thrilled by the level of support and funding received for her projects from both city and state. Her work was very personal and introspective until she and Warner Wada went to Northern Ireland to work on a friend's film. There they were swept up by the political anguish of Ireland. Together, she and Warner interviewed and photographed Irish people of all factions to produce *Control Zone*, a book and installation of photographs, paintings, and text representing people they encountered and their stories.

Donohue has since done other political photographic projects. She is currently working on a video filmed in South Africa with Morey Aronson, a South African. They posed as tourists speaking with and filming South Africans just before the government's information

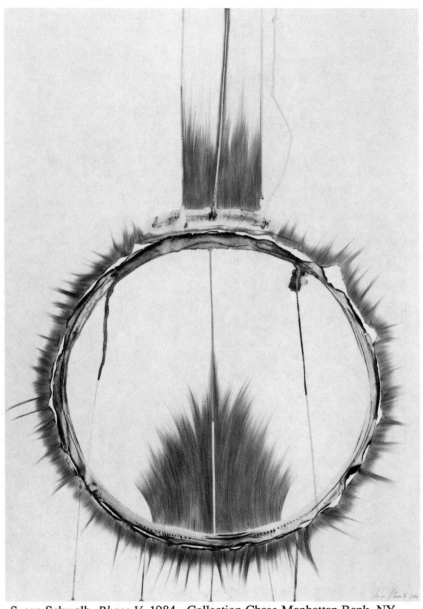

Susan Schwalb, *Phase V*, 1984. Collection Chase Manhattan Bank, NY.

Jeanne Lachance, *Hera's Hanging*.

blackout. Donohue told me she investigates "how politics affects individuals, how a person has to adjust his or her life, how people express themselves in an honest manner under oppressive conditions."

Photography as a journalistic tool has helped generate acceptance of political art photography, but not political art in general. **Laura Blacklow** of Cambridge, speaking about this dichotomy, concluded, "Most people want to see photographs look like the newspaper and drawings look like drawings." Blacklow's art is a combination of photography and drawing, using dream imagery. "I dream like Fellini makes films," she says. However, at a talk in 1984 for the Boston Women's Caucus for Art, she suggested that combining media made her work harder for people to accept.

Blacklow now works largely in book format. Initially a political decision: she wanted people to own art for little money. But she doesn't find the present time particularly difficult for political or confrontational art work. The art world has *never* wanted to be confronted with issues or politics, is the way she sees it.

Performance artist, graphic artist, and poet Jane Gillooly was born in Louisiana and came to Boston to attend the Massachusetts College of Art. Gillooly is interested in communication of images; that is, she develops images, then attempts to get them seen by people through mass media and reproducible formats. She has produced Xerox posters, artist's books, magazine illustrations, and most recently, slide/lecture/performance pieces.

Gillooly's work is based on personal vulnerability. By exploring personal experience, she gives a focus to political conditions. Like Bonnie Donohue, she is interested in how events affect people, in making the effects of social/political situations on individuals understandable to the viewer.

Gillooly's latest slide/lecture/performance work is about the Women's Prison in El Salvador. It is an astounding, profoundly moving story. Women inmates revolted and took over their prison using only sticks and rocks, to call attention to their situation. These women, interviewed and filmed in prison by Gillooly, had committed no crimes— they were simply picked up by the government and "disappeared." There are no charges against them, yet they are held with no hope of release.

Gillooly says the response to her work has been excellent, with many invitations to do perfomances in Boston and Cambridge. She also finds it easy to do political art in the Boston area, because there is such a large community of people active in concerns of conscience.

Judy Branfman, now a Boston artist, lived in Connecticut and New Hampshire. A fiber artist whose tapestry themes deal with women's issues, nuclear disarmament, and Central America, she organized an Artists' Delegation to Nicaragua in 1984 of New England artists and cultural workers. In 1985 she started a Connecticut Artists' Call against U.S. Intervention in Central America and has also participated in many other peace and Central American activites. Most of her work is commissioned and designed with a specific site in mind.

Connecticut artist **Ann Chernow**'s paintings are considered politically subversive by most viewers. Although she herself does not like to define them, she admits they deal with sexual politics. Ada Lambert, Associate Professor at Norwalk Community College, finds that Chernow's art "questions the nature of images of women and explores the sources of these pictorial representations and the assumptions which underlie them."[2]

Chernow paints images from Hollywood films, combining artistic, historical, and feminist elements. Hollywood films reinforce stereotypes of women by presenting them as truth. Chernow undermines these images of "cinema women," with paintings of film stills. As Lambert says, "She restores to women their humanity and individuality."

Ann Langdon of New Haven sent a statement about political art: "An artistic political statement may be as obvious as depicting a specific world political issue (e.g., South America) or as subtle— even unconscious— as a woman's finding a personal image that challenges the status quo of 'great' or 'good' art established by male-dominated art history." Langdon's work has fluctuated over time from representational to nonrepresentational and from painting to drawing. Her recent works are a series of torn, almost shredded canvases. She believes that although this work is more abstract and thus less aggressive in imagery, it still disturbs the viewer—"one of the foundations of political art" by her definition.

Pam Allara, art critic and art historian at Tufts University spoke about New England as an environment for creating political art. She characterized the art scene in Boston as one of general timidity, a reluctance to speak out. This attitude of course is not confined to Boston, perhaps partly because there has long been an elevated idea of art, a perception that art has to do with the mind solely, not political statement.

Finally, the lack of information about women artists who make political statements with their art may involve some confusion about what political art is. From the sample of artists I contacted, it seems that women artists frequently use personal experience to help define and explain social/political issues. Several people— artists and curators alike— were unsure if personal statements should be considered political. This uncertainty perhaps makes it more difficult for women to evolve a convenient accessible label or statement for their work. Or perhaps the real meaning of women artists' work is too subversive for the art world to accept.

Notes:
1. All statements not otherwise identified were received from this mailing.
2. See Ada Lambert, "The Art of Anne Chernow," *Hue Points*, Vol. xii (1983), p.13.

—**Linda Elwood**

Marcy Hermansader, *What Women Know About Weaving*, 1983.

THE ECONOMICS OF ART SURVIVAL
FOR NEW ENGLAND WOMEN

Feeling low lately but not quite sure why? Reluctant to buy those art supplies since your big commission fell through last month? Unable to sleep because you're worried about the rent? Convinced that you are the least successful artist in New England?

Take those stones out of your pockets, Virginia. Sit back, and read on, because the truth is out. Statistics prove that it is almost impossible to be an artist and a woman at the same time in New England, particularly if you are self-supporting. So if you have made it this far, still alive and artful, you are already way ahead of the game. You have survival skills beyond the wildest imagining of the world's economists.

A study released by the New England Foundation for the Arts in 1983 shows that the average net wage for women artists in Massachusetts is —$4.15 per hour. That is, *minus* $4.15! This means that after her costs are taken into account, the artist loses $4.15 for every hour she works on her art. In comparison, the average Massachusetts male artist's net hourly wage is +$1.53, nothing to crow about, yet $5.63 per hour more than the woman artist earns.[1]

Massachusetts has the bleakest figures. The picture brightens in New Hampshire, where a woman's net artistic wage is —$2.00 per hour. No net figures are available for Connecticut or Maine, while Vermont's numbers are almost positive —$0.03 per hour. If you've already begun to pack your suitcase, point yourself toward Rhode Island, where women seem to fare the best, +$2.79 per hour net artistic wages. [2]

This prodigious study provides nearly 200 pages of statistics and analyses regarding New England artists in the labor market. The four-page questionnaire was sent to a total of 17,653 artists in the six-state region; statistical results are based on 3,027 forms returned during 1980 and 1981. The study is significant, not only because of its scope, but because it begins to ask crucial questions within new frameworks. For instance, demographic groups include the following: Male , Female, American Indian, Asian, Black, White, and Hispanic. Nine different occupational classes of artists are included: Dancers, Musicians, Actors,

Theatre Production Personnel, Writers/Poets, Choreographers/
Composers/Playwrights, Visual Artists, Media Artists, and Craft
Artists.

If one assumes that the sampling is random and representative, some
morbidly fascinating facts emerge. There is a significant negative
relationship between years of education and artistic income; the more
educated the artist, the less likely she/he is to earn money by art-
making. Artists as a whole have a much higher level of educational
attainment than the average person in the New England labor force.
Over 80 percent of all artists have at least a bachelor's degree; the
regional average is 19.3 percent. Among artists there is no difference in
educational background between women and men, whites and non-
whites, except that women appear to begin their artistic training at a
slightly earlier age.

Three-quarters of the artists surveyed needed to hold additional jobs,
often more than one extra job at a time.   Women's secondary jobs paid
much less than men's. Furthermore, women were more likely than
men to be unemployed during the year; non-whites were more likely
than whites to be unemployed. Women were also less likely to collect
unemployment insurance. Women's most common reason listed for
being out of the labor force was "family obligations." Men's most
commonly listed reason was "improving artistic skills voluntarily."[3]

The limitations of this study are obvious but as yet unexplored.[4] We
see that women artists earn less per hour while working on their art and
less per hour while working at secondary jobs. We also find that they
are spending fewer hours per week on their art than men because of the
extra (underpaid) jobs and/or "family obligations." We are almost
convinced that unless there is another member of the household who
earns significantly more income than the woman artist, there is
virtually no way she can exist.

In short, after reading a study such as this, one marvels that there are
any women artists in New England at all.

But isn't this inquiry into " hourly wages" a rather crass
misrepresentation of an artist's mission in society? An artist, after all,
is much more than a maker of unmarketable "things." Surely, she is

-148-

more than the sum of her insolvent parts.

Alas, mission or none, profit or none, the rent must be paid. It is even more unfortunate that in New England — where so much that is wise and wonderful in American history seems to have been born — there is no firm tradition of women earning their own artistic way. Any notions about the economic aspects of being a woman in the arts, are deep-seated ones about the differences between "arts" and "crafts." These can be traced back through the nineteenth century in the context of New England's social and economic class structure.

Much has been written about the "art" and "craft" dichotomy in art history, generally, with evidence that perhaps in some previous age there was no difference between the two. This, however, was not the case in the nineteenth century in New England. In fact, particularly for women, "art" was for one economic stratum and "craft" for another. The unprivileged and working-class women learned weaving, quilting, knitting, clothing design, and other practical skills at home, in preparation for domestic roles as wife or servant. Wealthy women, on the other hand, learned sketching, painting, embroidery, music, and writing in environments where various other opportunitites were also opening up.[5] The women's college movement was based in New England; along with access to a classical education (a man's education, of sorts), the privileged women gained more visibility in public places. They were still held responsible, however, for the maintenance of domestic order and "beauty."[6]

Industrialization took its toll among the thousands of working class women in the New England mill towns. Handcrafted objects once valued at home and on the farm were mass-produced in factories. Economic necessity drove women to the mills, where they not only often worked in subhuman conditions but also lost control of the arts that had been their domain.

The high art/low art split corresponded to the pronounced stratification in New England society, and can be further traced in the educational opportunities available to these two estranged classes of women. In Boston during the 1870s the Massachusetts Normal Art School was established for training in the more practical arts.[7] The School of the

Museum of Fine Arts opened later in the same decade for a different group of students — the well born, well connected, and elegant. This period in Boston's history is often referred to as its Renaissance. Women artists connected with the Museum School at the time hardly resemble the women artists responding to the New England Foundation questionnaire in 1980. Instead of worrying about how to juggle two part-time jobs, child care, and a few harried hours of studio time, the nineteenth century woman who made fine art (painting, drawing, modeling, portraiture) had at least two residences and traveled around New England with her wealthy husband.[8]

Despite the stereotypes of women artists that emerge from available literature (most often written by men), we are nevertheless struck by two curious results of the art/craft dichotomy in New England women's art. Whatever the economic disparity between the two groups of women, the common denominator seems to be that neither group relied on art as a means of livelihood. Craft artists' work became either a form of unpaid domestic labor or a usurped, mass-produced commodity. Elitist painting and sculpture was made by wealthy practitioners who did not necessarily need to earn a living by it. Now that a middle class of women artists has emerged in the late twentieth century, with access to the same educational opportunities as male counterparts, women are still unable to support themselves through their own work. But there is no tradition for women to strive toward this end, and in New England, tradition is an important factor in approaching the world.

A second curious outcome is that the art/craft dichotomy seems never to have been fully resolved among New England women artists. Even though the original hierarchical associations — drudgery, repetition, and oppression on the one hand; elitism, superficiality, and empty ego on the other — even though these false dichotomies can now be seen as institutionalized notions imposed on women by outside forces, they appear to be deeply rooted and, alas, indigenous. Overly sensitized to this phenomenon, feminists have as hard a time as anyone trying to bridge the gap or to come up with fresh approaches to the problem.[9]

The arts are no longer a luxury for only the Brahmins, nor are they simply commodities that are poorly replicated and mass produced under oppressive factory conditions. Currently, the arts "industry" in New

England totals over $1.5 billion. The presence of artists creates thousands of jobs for people on the art-making periphery. Moreover, the arts are a significant factor in tourism, business relocation, and tax generation.[10] Although it is presently impossible to measure the economic impact of an individual artist, it is possible to wonder about the dollars she generates for other people. Has she become a cultural volunteer, rectifying the environment and enlightening the populace when she has a little spare time between wage-earning jobs?

The statistics may lead us astray. We do not need reminders that we earn —$4.15 per hour. We do need some way of asking each other how we have managed to exist thus far, how we have overcome the economic roadblocks and the effects of isolation. Granted, the study suffers some major conceptual and methodological flaws, but even a few questions dealing with women's experience would have enhanced the results.

What extraordinary problems do women of racial minorities face? How are single women artists faring? Where does women's emotional support come from — men, other women , close relatives? Do Lesbian artists have special economic problems, disadvantages or advantages? Do women experience much sexual harassment when they are working in the art business world, and does this have an economic effect? How much of women artists' time is spent in child care? How much "volunteer" art work is done for other groups, and can a dollar value be estimated for this unpaid work?

Who is this daring new woman artist, capable of living wisely and artfully against the greatest odds, with no real traditions to follow and few institutionalized networks of support?[11] May she resolve her differences among other women artists. Watch her barter for supplies and swap skills with other women. Let her seek out older women mentors. And finally, may she find a new breed of patron with an equal amount of courage and daring, who will cooperate in the development of new forms of "currency." May she never stop making art.

Notes:
1. Gregory Wassall, Neil Alper, and Rebecca Davison, *Art Work: Artists in the New England Labor Market.* (Cambridge: The New England Foundation for the Arts, 1983), p.119.
2. Ibid., with statistics cited on pp. 135, 173, and 155, respectively. The study also provides gross art hourly wages for women, before artistic costs are deducted: Massachusetts, $2.83 (men, $6.41), p.119; New Hampshire, $3.67 (men, $7.34), p.135; Connecticut, $3.44 (men, $7.61),p.84; Vermont, $5.06 (men, $5.30), p.173; Rhode Island, $6.92 (men, $8.73), p.155. There is no hourly breakdown available for Maine, although we are told that the "average artist" in Maine grossed $6.60, and in all artistic occupations (except crafts) male artists had higher wages than female artists. The differences ranged from 25 percent higher to 500 percent higher, depending on artistic category. However, in the case of crafts the average male craft artist earned almost $5.00 per hour net (see p.99).
3. Ibid., pp.42-47. The study's use of the term "unemployment" is a bit confusing. For instance, it states that someone can be dancing full-time but "unemployed" if not paid. On the other hand, a painter is "employed" if working on a painting in anticipation of selling it (see p.44).
4. See author's critique of the New England Foundation for the Arts *Art Work* study in *Women Artists News*, Volume 12, 1987. Another interesting statistical study conducted by the Friends Of Boston Art was coordinated by Nan Freeman. Although limited to the Boston area, and specifically addressing questions on adequate studio space, this 1986 survey found that 80 percent of all Boston artists earn less than $20,000 per year. Of that percentage, about 92 percent earn less than half of their income from art. Secondary jobs are held by 78 percent of all artists. Unfortunately, no demographic information about gender or race was solicited. These and other statistics from the Friends of Boston Art project are available at the Mayor's Office of Art and Humanities, Boston City Hall.(This city agency estimates that in Boston alone there are 14,000 artists.)
5. See Georgia Collins and Renée Sandell, *Women, Art, and Education*, (Reston, VA.: National Art Education Association,1984), p. 49, for an ambitious overview of this and other aspects of women's art education, here with specific references to Gordon S. Plummer, "Past and Present Inequities in Art Education" in Judy Loeb, ed., *Feminist Collage — Educating Women in the Visual Arts* (New York: Teachers College Press,

1979), pp.14-15, and Eleanor Flexner, *Century of Struggle: The Woman's Rights Movement in the United States.* (Cambridge: Harvard University Press, 1959, 1975), p.9.

6. A clear picture of this is given by Margaret Fuller in *Woman in the Nineteenth Century*, a book published in New York in 1845 as "a reproduction, modified and expanded" of an article published in *The Dial* in Boston, July, 1843. (The present edition was published in1971 by Norton and Company.) The "unpaid" aspect of this domestic work was fully explored by Charlotte Perkins Gilman in her *Women and Economics* (Boston: Small Maynard and Company, 1898, and New York: Harper and Row, 1966). Many 20th century feminist historians have explored this area of social history. Some excellent studies include: Barbara Welter, "The Cult of True Womanhood, 1820-1860," *American Quarterly*, XVIII, Summer, 1966: Nancy F. Cott, *The Bonds Of Womanhood:, "Women's Sphere"* in New England, 1780-1835, (New Haven: Yale University Press,1977); Adelle Simmons, "Education and Ideology in Nineteenth Century America: The Response of Educational Institutions to the Changing Role of Women, " and Ann D. Gordon and Mari Jo Buhle, "Sex and Class in Colonial and Nineteenth Century America," both in Berenice A. Carroll, Ed., *Liberating Women's History*, (Urbana: Univeristy of Illinois Press, 1976).

7. See Diana Korzenik, "The Art Education of Working Women, 1873-1903," in this volume.

8. Trevor J. Fairbrother, *The Bostonians : Painters of an Elegant Age, 1870-1930.* (Boston: Museum of Fine Arts, 1986), an exhibition catalog, with Boston exhibition dates June 11 - September 14, 1986. Mr. Fairbrother might not agree with this analysis. Of the 44 artists included in the exhibition, 10 are women, and not all of them are married. However, the catalog essays present a self-indulgent Boston, in which women artists play a minor part. Luckily, the artists' biographies written by Erica E. Hirshler give us some insight into the personal lives of the active women "fine artists" of this period.

9. In this context a controversy arose during the planning stages of the national exhibit for the1987 Women's Caucus for Art annual meeting. The Boston discussions revolved around the appropriateness of a craft-oriented theme such as "aprons" or "quilts" for a feminist audience. Interesting aspects of class bias among artists often are addressed in the work of Lucy Lippard. Good readings include "The Pink Glass Swan: Upward and Downward Mobility in the Art World," and "Making Something from Nothing (Toward a Definition of Womens' 'Hobby Art')."

both in Lippard's collection, *Get the Mesage? A Decade of Art for Social Change*, (New York: E.P. Dutton, 1984).

10. New England Foundation for the Arts, *The Arts and the New England Economy*, 2nd ed., (Cambridge: New England Foundation for the Arts, 1981), pp.33-49. The arts "industry" is defined to include nonprofit cultural organizations, educational institutions with arts programs, and the art audience.

11. For a fuller examination of this theme see Bonnie Woods, ""Historiogenic Art: Camouflage and Plumage," *Toward a Feminist Transformation of the Academy* (Ann Arbor: Great Lakes Colleges Association, 1979), pp.34-36.

—**Bonnie Woods**

Illustrations

Photo Credits:

E. Irving Blomstrann, p.13
eeva-inkeri, p.55
Geoffrey Clements, p. 54
Molly Upton, p.76
David Caras, p.82
Penelope Jencks, p.96
Cymie Payne, p.84
Dana Salvo, pp.110 and 121
Tom Lang, p.115
David Webber, p.122

William David Barry is a writer, historian, art critic, and exhibition consultant based in Portland, Maine. He has published widely in regional magazines and is the author of monographs, two books, and exhibition catalogs.

Pattie Chase is a fourth generation quiltmaker and quilt historian. She is the author of *The Contemporary Quilt: New American Quilts and Fabric* (E.P. Dutton, 1978), and has lectured extensively on contemporary quilts. In 1982 she co-directed the Cambridge Women's Quilt Project, a multi-ethnic enterprise, and in 1984 she curated an exhibition of 100 contemporary American quilts that traveled in Japan.

Doris Cole is president of Cole and Goyette, Architects and Planners, Inc. in Cambridge. Ms. Cole, a registered architect, has written several books including *From Tipi to Skyscraper: A History of Women in Architecture* and *Eleanor Raymond, Architect*. She is currently completing a book on Howe, Manning and Almy, Architects with co-author Karen Cord Taylor.

Linda Elwood is a Boston artist and illustrator who uses political imagery in her own works and is interested in investigating its forms and scope in the work of New England artists. She has had several solo exhibitions in New York and Boston.

Alicia Faxon is Associate Professor of Art History at Simmons College. She instituted and teaches a History of Women Artists course and has written numerous articles on women artists for *Woman's Art Journal* and *Women Artists News*, as well as articles on nineteenth century art for *The Art Bulletin*, *The Metropolitan Museum of Art Journal*, *Master Drawings*, and *The Print Collector's Newsletter*. Her latest book is *Jean-Louis Forain: A Catalogue Raisonné of the Prints* (1982).

Johanna Gill is Chair of the Media and Peforming Arts Department and Associate Professor of Art History at Massachusetts College of Art. She has published on video art and on a wide range of contemporary art topics.

Bonnie Grad is Associate Professor of Art History at Clark University. She has curated several museum exhibitions and written their catalogs, among them, *Visions of City and Country: Prints and Photographs of Nineteenth Century France* (with Timothy Riggs, 1982), and *Milton Avery Monotypes* (1977). Her articles have appeared in *Art New England, The Print Collector's Newsletter*, and other publications.

Virginia Gunter, a sculptor, has exhibited widely in the Boston area and appears in *Contemporary American Women Sculptors* by Virginia Watson-Jones, (Oryx, 1986). She has written about sculpture and curated the Boston Museum of Fine Arts centennial exhibition, *Earth, Air, Fire ,Water: Elements of Art.*.

Erica Hirshler, Research Assistant at the Department of Paintings of the Boston Museum of Fine Arts, recently assisted in the organization of the exhibition *The Bostonians* at the museum, contributing 96 biographies to the catalog.

Diana Korzenik is chair of the Department of Art Education at Massachusetts College of Art and has written a number of articles on art education. Her recently published book, *Drawn to Art*, winner of the 1986 Winship Award, shows how drawing became an important element in nineteenth century American education.

Dorothy Mayhall is Director of Art at the Stamford Museum and Nature Center, Connecticut. She formerly directed the Aldrich Museum of Contemporary Art, Ridgefield, Connecticut, and the Storm King Center, Mountainville, New York.

Sylvia Moore is an editor of college textbooks at Prentice-Hall. She writes frequently on contemporary women's art and is co-editor of *Women Artists of the World*.

Penny Redfield recently served an internship at the Bostonian Society doing research on needlework and needlework schools. She discovered not only a number of interesting needlework examples, but also much material proving the importance of such work in the education of young women.

Helen S. Shlien has a long standing interest in performance and installation art. She is a former gallery owner and director and has curated many exhibitions of contemporary art. She is the author of *Artists Associations in the U.S.A.*, and has been an active member of the Boston Visual Artists Union since its founding.

Leslie Sills has been a sculptor in ceramics since the early 1970s. Her most recent exhibitions have been at the Clark Gallery in Lincoln and the Berkshire Art Museum in Pittsfield, Massachusetts. She was founder and director of the Children's Creative Clay Studio School, and taught there from 1976 to 1982. Active in the Boston Women's Caucus for Art, she served as co-chair in 1984-85.

Sarah Sutro, a Somerville artist, 1986-87 chair of the Boston Women's Caucus, has exhibited in Boston, New York, and London. She is Artist-in-Residence at the Cultural Educational Collaborative of Boston, and teaches at the DeCordova Museum School.

Bonnie Woods, a Boston artist, has exhibited nationally, published on the subject of feminism in the visual arts, and served on a variety of art panels.

Design and Typography: William Bowles

Cover design by Two Lip Art.
Cover photo: class of EWD Hamilton, 1894, courtesy
Massachusetts College of Art Library Archives.